Dedicated to my son-in-law Jörn

1st English edition 1999

© of the German edition
Werner Gitt: Faszination Mensch
1996 by CLV · Christliche Literatur-Verbreitung
Postfach 110135 · D-33661 Bielefeld, Germany
© of the English edition
1999 by CLV · Christliche Literatur-Verbreitung
Postfach 110135 · D-33661 Bielefeld
Translation: Prof. Dr Jaap Kies, Dr Carl Wieland,
            Dörte Götz, Veronika Abraham
Corrections: Dr Carl Wieland
Typography: Enns Schrift & Bild, Bielefeld
Cover and Design: Dieter Otten, Gummersbach
Printed in Germany: by GGP

ISBN 3-89397-397-4

The Wonder of Man

dlv

Christliche Literatur-Verbreitung e.V.
Postfach 11 01 35 · 33661 Bielefeld · Germany

Contents

Part 2   What is man?

Foreword

What would you expect from a book called *The Wonder of Man*? In German the title is *Faszination Mensch*. What fascinates you – what do you see as wonderful? The work of some great painter, a virtuoso singer or musician? Or perhaps it is a sensational athletic achievement, or some marvellous technological advance.

This book is concerned with the general question: What is man? What *is* a human being? A science writer gave the following answer:

"Man is a wonderful, inconceivably complex being. Consider the facts: A chemical factory, an electrical network, climate control, filtration plant – all these controlled centrally by the brain, a thinking computer with the additional ability of loving and hating. Our organism keeps itself alive for several decades, and through various control mechanisms, operates almost without friction. We consist of a hundred million million microscopic parts, all of which are fantastically fine-tuned to, and co-operatively integrated with, each other. When healthy, these parts are continuously rejuvenated and can even repair themselves.

"This entire marvellous body is kept in operation by a fist-sized pump, the heart, which beats 100,000 times a day and transports nourishment throughout the entire body by means of five litres of blood. The volume of air passing through our lungs during the course of a day is about 20,000 litres. This provides the necessary oxygen, and the unwanted gases are exhaled at the same time. The normal operating temperature is 37 degrees Celsius. Unfortunately, like everything else, it is subject to wear and tear.

"The human body can be investigated with a magnification factor of 200,000 by means of electron microscopes, which enable us to observe nearly all its deepest recesses."

Some of the aspects mentioned above warrant closer consideration. In this book we won't concern ourselves with the body of some special person of extraordinary ability and achievement, but with the faculties we all have in common. We will take a closer look at just some of the wonderful and ingeniously planned details of the human body. You will be amazed, to say the least, and a little thought will lead you to some vitally important conclusions.

Plan of this book: There are two main parts. In the first, many amazing details of the human body are presented, showing that we are wonderfully made. This automatically leads to the question: Whose plans and ideas are incorporated in this wonderful construction; who made us?

There are essentially only two possible answers: Either I am the result of blind physical and chemical processes planned by nobody, or I was made by an incredibly brilliant Creator. A closer look at the human body can help us to come to the appropriate conclusion.

The many numbers given in the first part for various values require a note of clarification: Textbooks and scientific articles often give divergent values for these. This is firstly because there is so much variation between individuals. Also, because many of the numbers are so large (e.g. the number of cells in the body), they can only be estimated or calculated indirectly. So it is not surprising that the numbers vary from source to source.

In the second part of the book we discuss questions about the essence of man: Why are we like we are? Why do we behave as we do? Why has no ideology succeeded in improving man? What is our future? Is death the end of everything? Is there an eternity? If so – what can we expect?

While the first part emphasises scientific knowledge, in the second part the Bible takes a more central role. Bible quotes are from the New International Version except where otherwise stated.

Readership and purpose of this book: No special readership is intended. The many amazing details of the human frame will likely interest everyone, regardless of age, level of education, gender, or occupation. In this book scientific facts are linked to biblical affirmations. The main purpose of the book is to bring seekers, doubters, atheists and agnostics to faith. By faith is not meant some vague, universal religious impulse, but true saving faith in the Redeemer, Jesus Christ. For this reason the necessary space is devoted to explaining both the necessity of redemption and the way of salvation. Those who follow through will indeed see the wonder and fascination of not only the facts about their own selves, but also by the amazing Creator Who made us and told us through his prophet: "Since you are precious and honored in my sight, and because I love you..." (Is 43:4).

Acknowledgement and thanks: After discussing everything with my wife, as usual, the manuscript was scrutinised by Dr Jutta Nemitz (Braunschweig) and by Andreas Wolff (Giessen). My son-in-law, Jörn Becker (Bonn) and staff of the CLV-Verlag did the final editing. Our son, Carsten, prepared some cartoons concerning our sense organs. I am grateful to all involved for their valued assistance. Finally, I thank CLV-Verlag for their constructive critiques and pleasant cooperation in the production of this illustrated publication.

Werner Gitt

Additional foreword to the English edition

As author, I am delighted that this book is now appearing in the English language. The initial strenuous work of translation was done by Prof. Dr Jaap Kies (South Africa). He was assisted in translation of the many technical medical terms by Dr Desmond Stumpf and Dr Johannes Steinberg. Rudolf Steinberg Pr. Eng. was of great support by looking up the original English citations in libraries, where the text originated from a translation into German.

The main purpose of the book is to win people for heaven. It is thus necessary to explain the nature of heaven in some detail. The original German book only devoted two pages to this central theme, so for the English version, these were replaced with a substantially expanded section. I am thankful to Dörte Götz, MA, for translating this chapter. She has a degree in English and Russian translation from the University of Heidelberg (Germany). Veronika Abraham, pursuing studies towards a BA in History and Philosophy at Queen's University in Canada, also helped with translating this chapter. Sarah Jayne Curtius, BA, was born in Britain and completed German and English language studies in Sheffield. She has reviewed this chapter stylistically, making refinements where necessary.

Finally, my friend Dr Carl Wieland (Australia) went through the entire translated manuscript in detail, checking against the original and correcting as necessary from both a medical and stylistic viewpoint, as well as translating a number of additional sections I provided for the various chapters. Dr Wieland is the director of the world-renowned organisation for creation science/research, "Answers in Genesis" in Brisbane (Australia). He is editor of their brilliantly presented and colourful English-language magazine "Creation ex Nihilo" (print run > 50,000) which has subscribers in more than 120 countries.

To all who have helped in any way in bringing about the publication of this edition, I extend my warmest thanks.

Werner Gitt   November 1998

Part 1: Man – an ingenious construction

Our sense organs

– brilliantly designed tools for perception

Our senses are our windows on the external world. Only via this 'radar network' of our senses can we observe, recognise, experience and understand our world. Our senses determine the quality of our conscious life, and influence many of our decisions. Input from our senses can trigger a wide range of emotions in us; for example joy, happiness, peace and contentment, but also pain, fear, anger and sorrow.

We can extend the limits of our sensory capacities by means of technological aids like microscopes, telescopes, and stethoscopes. Our senses are on a continual voyage of discovery. A large part of our lives is spent on treating our senses to new, special experiences. We undertake long journeys to visit new countries, so as to experience distant deserts, mountains, lakes or beaches. We visit the zoo, movies or the theatre; we listen to classical music or pop concerts, buy exotic perfumes, or spend money on culinary delights. Whenever we willingly pay high admission fees, it is because we want to give our senses some special treat.

Clearly, the quality of our human experience is in large measure determined by our senses. So we will take an extensive look at not only the many abilities of our sense organs, but also the details of their construction.

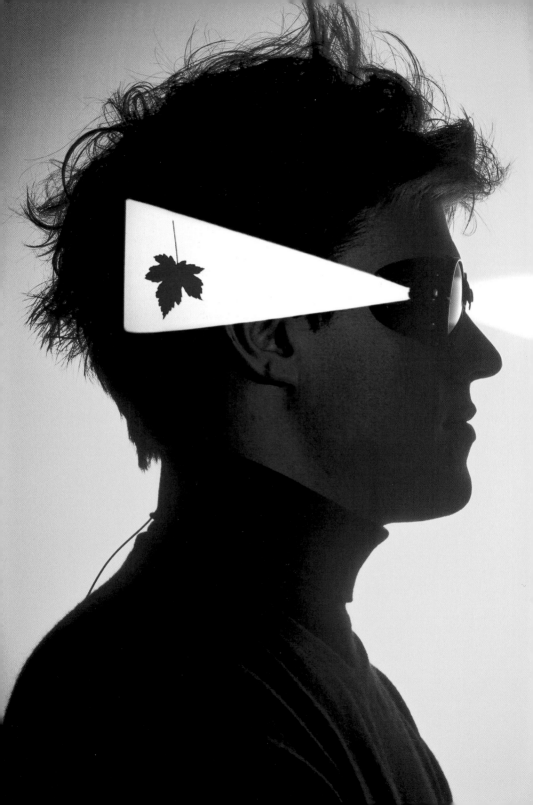

The eye

– our window to the outside

We read in the Bible that "The eye never has enough of seeing" (Eccl 1:8). The eye is actually one of our most important sense organs, since well over half of all the information we take in about our surroundings comes to us by way of our eyes. Through being able to perceive incident light, we can read letters, newspapers, and books; marvel at the colours of a blossom, the perspectives of a landscape, the beauty of a dress, or the artistic appeal of a painting. But especially, we can see our loved ones and others whom we encounter in our daily lives. The German word for face is *Gesicht* which means the same as vision or sight. The English (and French) word *visage*, also meaning face, similarly refers to seeing (from the Latin *videre* = to see).

Physiologically speaking, seventy percent of all our sense receptors are located in the eyes. In reality, we evaluate and understand our world mostly from being able to see it. That's why, despite all their differences, all human languages are rich in visual imagery. Figures of speech and proverbs, though conveying abstract meanings, are often easily visualised, like: "Up to one's neck in debt"; "Carrying your heart on your sleeve"; "A rolling stone gathers no moss".

In the Bible, the Creator commanded on the very first day: "Let there be light!" Our visual sense was thus provided for right from the beginning. When He reviewed His creative works, we read five times: "And God saw that it was good." In reviewing all He had made at the end of the six creation days, we again find His evaluation based on vision: "And God saw all that he had made, and it was very good" (Gen 1:31).

Having established the importance of vision, we now turn to the actual organ of sight.

General features of the eye: Visible light comprises electromagnetic radiation with wavelengths between 400 (violet) and 750 (red) nanometres (1 nm = 10^{-9} m = one millionth of a millimetre). For the purpose of forming an image, the incident light rays must be bent (refracted) and focused sharply on the retina. The cornea handles most of the refraction and the lens subsequently focuses images at various distances by varying its curvature. Through this ingeniously devised ability to change its shape, the focal length of the lens can vary between 69.9 mm and 40.4 mm. This is why, unlike the best products of the optical industry, we can manage with only one lens.

The iris acts like the diaphragm of a camera. There are two opposing sets of muscles which regulate the size of the aperture (the pupil) according to the brightness of the light. The shape of the eye is maintained by the vitreous body, and the pressure in a fluid called the aqueous humour which fills the anterior and posterior chambers. This pressure depends on a balance between the production of this fluid and its outflow. The cornea is lubricated, and protected against drying out, by the tear ducts and the movements of the eyelids.

Of all our sense organs, our eyes have the greatest range of detection sensitivity, as well as the greatest adaptability. They have their own machinery of movement, through special muscles which enable vision to be directed towards a target. The two-dimensional image on the retina requires massive parallel processing in the subsequent network of nerve fibres.

Structure of the eye: The eye can be divided functionally into two parts, namely the physical dioptric mechanism (Greek: *dioptra* = something through which one looks) which handles incident light, and the receptor area of the retina where the light triggers processes in nerve cells. The dioptric mechanism produces a miniaturised, upside down image. To obtain a sharp image requires an exact "fine tuning" between the refractory (light-bending) properties of the optical medium and the dimensions of the eye. A deviation in the latter as small as 0.1 mm is enough to cause faulty vision, requiring correction by spectacles.

The cornea's main task is to protect the delicate components of the eye against damage by foreign bodies. The iris is located between the cornea and the lens, and its function is to control the amount of incident light, in the same way as the diaphragm of a camera. The lens focuses the incoming light rays on to the retina (Latin: *rete* = net), where the actual process of perception begins. The photo-receptors (the rods and cones) convert the incident 'optical signals' into chemical (and subsequently into electrical) signals. These electrical signals then travel to the brain along the optic nerve. There are no photo-receptor cells at the point where the optic nerve leaves the retina, and this is known as the "blind spot". Another important feature of the retina is the so-called "yellow spot" (the *macula lutea*). In the middle of

this is the *fovea centralis*, the point where visual acuity is at a maximum. There are no rods in this position, only cones, which are connected in a special way to the relevant nerve cells. When you focus your attention on a certain object, your head and eyes automatically move in such a way as to let its image fall on the fovea for greatest sharpness.

The retina: The back of the eye can be observed through the pupil using an ophthalmoscope. The retina, with the blood vessels supplying its inner layers, can be seen, as well as the blind spot and the yellow spot.

The retina plays a key role in visual perception. This thin (only 0.2 mm) layer of nerve tissue lines

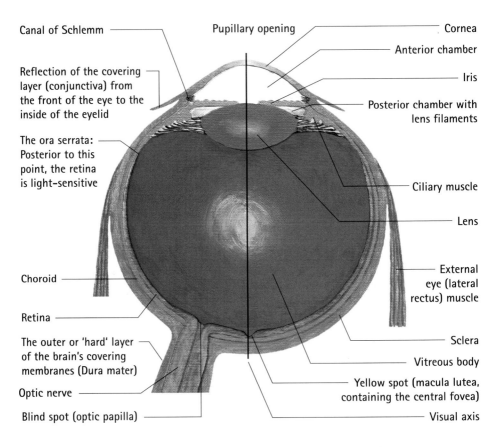

Canal of Schlemm

Pupillary opening

Cornea

Anterior chamber

Reflection of the covering layer (conjunctiva) from the front of the eye to the inside of the eyelid

Iris

Posterior chamber with lens filaments

The ora serrata: Posterior to this point, the retina is light-sensitive

Ciliary muscle

Lens

Choroid

External eye (lateral rectus) muscle

Retina

The outer or 'hard' layer of the brain's covering membranes (Dura mater)

Sclera

Vitreous body

Optic nerve

Yellow spot (macula lutea, containing the central fovea)

Blind spot (optic papilla)

Visual axis

Transverse view of the right human eye
(after Faller/Schünke, *Der Körper des Menschen*, Thieme-Verlag)

the inside of the eyeball. It contains the photo-receptor (light-sensitive) cells and four types of nerve cells, as well as structural cells and epithelial pigment cells (Latin: *pigmentum* = dye; Greek: *epithel* = outer layer of the skin). The two kinds of photo-cells are called rods and cones because

of their shape. These microscopically small light detectors, which contain the various visual pigments, are masterpieces of technological efficiency. Each eye has about 110 million rods and 6 million cones. They form a laterally interconnected network and are connected "vertically", by means of so-called bipolar cells, to the one million ganglion cells. These collect all the optical signals received by the retina, determine the direction of flow of these signals, and transmit them to the brain through the optic nerve. This bundle of more than one million nerve fibres, each well "insulated" from the others, is about 2 mm thick. Present-day communications experts using glass fibre technology can only dream of a "cable" of this kind.

One single square millimetre of the retina contains approximately 400,000 optical sensors. To get some idea of such a large number, imagine a sphere, on the surface of which circles are drawn, the size of tennis balls. These circles are separated from each other by the same distance as their diameter. In order to accommodate 400,000 such circles, the sphere must have a diameter of 52 metres, nearly three times as large as the hot air balloons used for advertising promotions.

The photo-receptors: The rods and cones not only differ in shape, but also in function. The rods are cylindrical, while the cones are smaller and have a tapered form. In the case of low illumination as at night, the rods enable us to dis-

tinguish between brightness and darkness. They are so sensitive that the absorption of a single photon results in a measurable electrical signal. This high sensitivity is achieved through having a long time lag (about 0.3 seconds) between the absorption of a photon and the emission of the electric signal, allowing a complex amplification process to take place.

The cones operate much faster; their time lag is only 0.075 seconds, but they are much less sensitive than the rods, and only function optimally in daylight. There are three types of cones, distinguished by their absorption maxima, each being most sensitive for, respectively, red light (having a wave length of approximately 705 nm), green light (520 nm), and blue light (450 nm). By comparing the messages received from the different cones, the ganglia identify the colours actually observed.

We would expect the light receptors to be on the side of the retina exposed to the incident light, but, amazingly, this is not the case. The light must first pass through another layer of the retina. That is why it has been said that our eyes have "inverted wiring", an arrangement which nevertheless works brilliantly.

The light sensitive cells act like interpreters, translating the impulses of light into the language of the nervous system. Another way of putting it is that a photo-receptor cell is basically a counter which counts the number of incident light quanta (photons). Its sensitivity ranges over five powers of ten, and it is able to adapt to the brightness of the prevailing light conditions by altering its sensitivity. For example, in response to bright light, it can reduce its sensitivity 100,000 times!

Sensitivity: We are blessed with extremely sensitive sense organs. Furthermore, the Creator solved a universal technical problem. Whenever a radio receiver is set for maximum sensitivity, it becomes noisy. This hissing sound is caused by the irregular thermal (heat) motions of electrons in the resistors. It can be eliminated by cooling all the components to a temperature far below freezing. But this is impractical, and is technically impossible for signals having the same strength as the (statistical) noise. A certain trick helps – transmit the signal on two separate channels and subsequently combine them. In this way the random noise fluctuations in each partially cancel each other out, resulting in an appreciable reduction in noise.

This method is also employed in the eye. In sensory organs and nerve cells, "noise" is not so much a result of fluctuations in electron density, but is caused by fluctuations in the voltage on the interfaces between sensory and nerve cells. The Creator made our optic cells as sensitive as physically possible. As mentioned, one single light quantum (photon), the smallest physical unit of light, is sufficient to cause an electric impulse in an optic cell. Any possible illusion which might be caused by "noise", is eliminated as follows:

Several hundred rods, the most highly sensitive cells, are connected to only one nerve cell. These special nerve cells only transmit an impulse if a sufficiently strong signal has been received from at least four or five optic cells within a certain time period, about 0.02 seconds. This means that the *individual* optic cells are as sensitive as at all physically possible, but the nervous system only transmits signals when several impulses arrive more or less at the same moment, after a certain summation period. Thus the maximum possible sensitivity only comes into play when the light stimulus arises virtually simultaneously from receptor cells spread over a sizeable area, and not from just a single point. Random "noise" fluctuations would arise at different times in each cell, so are never transmitted.

Visual acuity: Visual acuity (sharpness), the ability to resolve objects, is very important in the assessment of vision. Under good illumination a normal eye can distinguish between two points if the incident light rays make an angle of 1 minute (1' = 1/60 degree).

Adaptation (Latin: *adaptio* = adjustment, especially that of sensory organs to the prevailing

conditions): Our eyes are able to process bright and dim light over a wide range. At night we can observe dim stars, and we can also adapt to the glaring intensity of bright sunlight reflected from snow and ice. This amazing adaptability of the eye spans an immense range – a factor of 1 to 1 million million!

Colour perception: We would have missed something wonderful if we could not see colours! Colours may bring joy, and can even affect our moods. They contribute to happiness and affect our state of mind. Colours fascinate all of us, not just artists and fashion designers.

Colours can be characterised by three aspects, namely hue, brightness, and saturation (= the degree of admixture with white). Our eyes can distinguish 300 different hues or shades of colour, and if, in addition, the brightness and saturation are varied as well, several million possible colour values can be distinguished. The brightness of a colour is determined by the strength of illumination, and the saturation.

In our eyes it is only the cones which can detect colours. The chemical involved is called rhodopsin (Greek *rhodon* = a rose), or visual purple. It consists of protein molecules (comprising approximately 350 amino acids), including the so-called retinal which colours the rhodopsin. Retinal also makes the rhodopsin sensitive to light, similar to the way a detonator makes a cartridge sensitive to being struck by a firing pin. The rhodopsin of a cone cannot absorb all the light quanta (photons) which strike it; it "selects" quanta of a certain size (wavelength). It will capture most or all of such quanta, but will also capture one out of ten to one out of fifty of those which are exactly double or half the preferred size. However, each photon captured has the same effect, regardless of the wavelength.

There are three types of cones, each preferring a specific, optimal quantum size. They are known respectively as red-, green-, or blue-sensitive cones, according to the optical pigments and the preferred quantum size (wavelength of the incoming photons of light). But all this still does not mean that we can see colours – it only provides the necessary preconditions.

The sensation of colour only arises in the brain after a computational comparison of the excitation of the three types of cones. There are about 100 million optic cells in the retina, but only one million optic nerve fibres lead from them. This means that many optic cells are interconnected in a complex fashion. The optic nerve transmits image information to various parts of the brain in the form of electrical pulses. A small number of fibres lead directly to the mid-brain, but most of them converge on a switchboard which serves the primary vision centre in the rear of the brain.

The images formed on both retinas are upside down and also left-right inverted. But an astounding fact is that the optic nerves from both eyes split up and cross each other in such a way that the left halves of the images of both eyes are received by the right half of the brain, and the right halves end up in the left hemisphere of the brain. Each half of the observer's brain receives information from only one half of the image. In addition, these images are distorted, because the region around the yellow spot (the *fovea* – where we see best; the Latin word for a hollow) forms an image which is ten times as large as that of the peripheral area. The left side of the brain only observes the left half of the image (= the right half of what we are looking at) and this half is the right way up with the distortion removed. At the same time the right side of the brain deals with the other half of the field of view.

Note that, although the brain processes the different parts of the image in various remote locations, the two halves of the field of vision are seamlessly re-united, without any trace of a joint – amazing! This process is still far from being fully understood.

Hermann von Helmholtz (1821 – 1894), a famous physicist and physiologist of the 19th century, comparing the error count of eye imaging with that of a lens, concluded as follows in 1863:

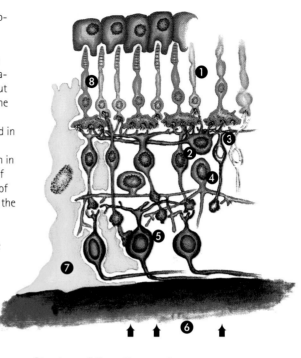

Structure of the retina

① Rods
② Horizontal cells
③ Bipolar cells
④ Amacrine cells
⑤ Ganglia
(singular = ganglion)
⑥ Direction of incident light
⑦ Glial (supporting) cells
⑧ Cones

"If an optician sold me an instrument having the errors exhibited by the eye, it would be in order for me to express my dissatisfaction with the quality of his work in the strongest terms, and return his instrument forthwith."

Helmholtz was wrong, since he only measured the performance of the lens of the eye in comparison with the light path in optical instruments. But he forgot that no technologically produced lens system can function faultlessly for the length of a human lifespan. Neither is it protected against heat and cold, dryness and humidity, shocks and dust, nor can it repair itself in the event of minor damage. Which optical instrument available at that time could adjust itself automatically to prevailing conditions like bright-dark contrasts, distance, and the light spectrum? And which optical system processes the data prior to transmitting it to a computer, like the eye? But remember that, as we shall see later, the brain is much more than a computer.

The Bible and the eye: All evolutionary statements about the origin of the eye notwithstanding, the Bible affirms unequivocally that the eye is uniquely the work of the Creator. Its conception and complexity defy human genius. We read in Psalm 94:9: "Does he who formed the eye not see?" If this Word is true, as I am deeply convinced it is, then any other human ideas and words about the origin of the eye are wrong from the outset.

The eye is described in the Bible as a very important organ. It cannot become satisfied (Prov 27:20), and our heart follows our eyes (Job 31:7). The German proverb "What the eye sees, the heart believes", is derived from this fact. Being a mirror of our soul, our eyes strongly express our personality. In the Sermon on the Mount, Jesus described this truth: "The eye is the lamp of the body. If your eyes are good, your whole body will be full of light. But if your eyes are bad, your whole body will be full of darkness. If then the light within you is darkness, how great is that darkness!" (Matt 6:22-23).

Many other biblical statements confirm that the eye expresses our innermost nature – aspects like generosity (Prov 22:9), pride and haughtiness (Ps 18:27; 131:1, Prov 6:17, and Is 10:12), idolatry (Ez 6:9), and adultery (2 Peter 2:14). Our eyes can be piercing with hatred (Job 16:9), winking with malice (Ps 35:19), or closed to the poor and needy (Prov 28:27). With our eyes we marvel at God's works (Ps 118:23) and expect help from Him: "I lift up my eyes to you, to you whose throne is in the heaven. As the eyes of slaves look to the hand of their master, as the eyes of a maid look to the hand of her mistress, so our eyes look to the LORD our God, till he shows us his mercy" (Ps 123:1-2). When looking up to God, we expect his help: "I lift up my eyes to the hills – where does my help come from? My help comes from

the LORD, the Maker of heaven and earth" (Ps 121:1-2).

When man fell into sin, the eyes played a significant role: "the woman *saw* that the fruit of the tree was good for food and *pleasing to the eye*" (Gen 3:6). The eye was the gate to sin. Samson also experienced this. His downfall was caused by his marrying a heathen woman. What decided him, was her visible attractiveness: "She's the right one for me" (Judges 14:3b).

Our salvation also has to do with vision. Jesus came to this world and He could be seen by human eyes. The pious Israelite Simeon had received a promise that he would not die before seeing Christ the Lord. When he held the baby Jesus in his arms, he praised God and said "... my *eyes* have *seen* your salvation" (Luke 2:30).

The apostle John expressed his knowledge of Jesus as an eye-witness: "We have *seen* his glory, the glory of the One and Only, who came from the Father, full of grace and truth" (John 1:14). And the salient feature of His second coming is that everybody will *see* Him: "Look, he is coming with the clouds, and every eye will *see* him, even those who pierced him; and all the peoples of the earth will mourn because of him" (Rev 1:7). On that day everybody will see Him, either as Saviour or as Judge.

With enlightened eyes – such enlightenment is also a gift of God – we can know His glory and wisdom (Eph 1:17-18). And what God has prepared for us in heaven is rich and vast beyond comprehension, as described in 1 Corinthians 2:9: "No eye has seen, no ear has heard, no mind has conceived what God has prepared for those who love Him." Heaven is the destination of the redeemed, and when we arrive there, we will *see* the Lord Jesus as He is (1 John 3:2b). In this world many people suffer severe pain and misery, and the question "Why?" is cried out often. But when we arrive at our destination, everything will be made clear, because Jesus said: "In that day you will no longer ask me anything" (John 16:23). All suffering will end, as stated in Revelation 21:4: "He (God) will wipe every *tear from their* eyes. There will be no more death or mourning or crying or pain, for the old order of things has passed away."

Quotes:

Charles Darwin (1809 – 1882) in his book *The Origin of the Species*:

"To suppose that the eye with all its inimitable contrivances for adjusting the focus to different distances, for admitting different amounts of light, and for the correction of spherical and chromatic aberration, could have been formed by natural selection, seems, I freely confess, absurd in the highest degree."

Dr. Carl Wieland, M.B., B.S., in the magazine *Creation ex nihilo* (Vol. 18, No. 2, 1996, p. 40):

"Eyes in different creatures are designed to meet their differing needs. Humans need good resolution and detail, whereas a fly needs speed. We see a fluorescent lamp as flickering at 10 Hz (cycles per second) but it looks stable to us at 20 Hz. A fly can detect a flicker of 200 Hz, so a normal movie would look to it like a slide show! The simple act of walking into a room and immdiately recognizing all the objects in it requires more computing power than a dozen of the world's top supercomputers put together."

Proverb:
"There are none so blind as those who will not see."

French author Antoine de Saint-Exupéry (1900 – 1944):
"One can only see well through one's heart."

Units of length:
1 kilometre = 1 km = 1000 m
1 metre = 1 m = 100 cm
1 centimetre = 1 cm = 10 mm = 10^{-2} m
1 millimetre = 1 mm = one thousandth
                          of a metre
1 mm = 1000 µm = 10^{-3} m
1 micrometre = 1 µm = one thousandth
                          of a millimetre
1 µm = 1000 nm = 10^{-6} m
1 nanometre = 1 nm = one millionth
                          of a millimetre
1 nm = 1000 pm = 10^{-9} m
1 picometre = 1 pm = one thousand millionth
                          of a millimetre
1 pm = 0.001 nm = 10^{-12} m

20

The ear

– our highest-precision sense organ

Without the sense of hearing we would lack an important method of orientation. Like a bird in a small cage, we would then be largely excluded from everyday events,. Sounds intensify the sensory impressions of life. We can listen to the murmur of rippling wavelets at our feet, while at the same time hearing the booming of the mighty breakers rolling in from the ocean. When taking a stroll, we enjoy the humming of bees flitting from blossom to blossom, as well as the exuberant song of a lark. We can hear a wide range of sounds, from the soft whining of a mosquito to the ear-shattering noise of a jet plane taking off. The racket of pneumatic drills and other noisy machines are also part of our everyday experience. Although these sound signals reveal their origin, they do not convey any personal messages to us.

In addition to receiving sounds, we can also transmit them. Speaking and hearing comprise our basic method of communication. In this case the kinds of noises and their significance are completely different. Musical notes, songs, and the spoken word bear meaningful messages. The act of identifying their inherent meaning involves much more than merely processing the received sound waves. A special evaluation system, located in the brain, is required for this purpose. Without the brain we would not have been able to hear. Our souls are stirred by what we hear, as expressed by the poignant French proverb: "The ear is the way to the heart."

In our contact with the world our sense of hearing is just as important as our vision. Sounds are air vibrations which are detected by our ears, where they are first converted into hydro-dynamic vibrations, and subsequently into electrical nerve impulses. Finally the brain identifies these signals as information.

Did you know that the human ear is a detection device which utilises a level of technology that no science has as yet been able to attain, or even (in many aspects) to understand? For the purpose of describing this, we need a few technical terms, which will first be explained:

Sound level: Vibrating objects (like a tuning fork, the cone of a loudspeaker, or human vocal chords) induce vibrations in the surrounding air. Adjacent air molecules are accelerated, causing waves travelling at a speed of approximately 330 m/s. This phenomenon is called sound, and in a sound field there are zones where air molecules are more densely packed than in other zones. Air pressure is greater in the denser zones, and smaller in the less dense zones. Sound vibrations can be depicted as wave-shaped graphs. The distance between two adjacent locations where the air pressure is the same, is known as the wave length. The maximum deviation from the neutral value is called the amplitude. If the wave length increases (implying a decrease in the number of vibrations per time unit), the pitch of the sound becomes lower. And, vice versa, when

① The curved rim of the helix forms a tunnel or flume
② The root of the helix (Crus helicus)
③ Concealed opening of the external acoustic meatus
④ Lid of the ear (Tragus)
⑤ Antitragus
⑥ Concha (a hollow depression)
⑦ Antihelix
⑧ Helix
⑨ Gateway to the flume of the helix
⑩ Darwin's tubercle

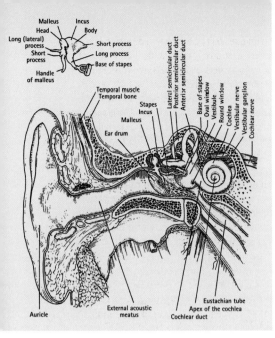

Structure of the human ear.

Sound vibrations travel through the external acoustic meatus to the ear drum, and then via the malleus, the incus, and the stapes through the oval window into the liquid-filled cochlea. The round window allows the pressure between the cochlea and the air-filled middle ear to be equalised. The three arc-shaped structures (semi-circular ducts) are part of the organ of balance. Sounds are detected in the two spirals of the cochlea which contain the organ of Corti. This has some 15,000 sensory "hair" cells. A thick "cable" of nerve fibres (the cochlear branch of the 8th cranial nerve), leads from the cochlea to the brain.

the number of vibrations per time unit increases (shorter wave length), we hear a higher pitched sound. The pitch of a tone – its frequency – is measured in Hertz (1 Hz = one vibration per second). If the amplitude increases, the sound becomes louder, and a decrease in amplitude results in a softer sound. Everyday sounds comprise a mixture of different frequencies and amplitudes.

The amplitude of a sound is called sound pressure, which, in the same way as any other type of pressure, can be measured in N/m² (Newtons per square metre). But in acoustics, another unit is preferred, called sound level or noise level, which is measured in dB (deciBels). To convert sound pressure p_x into the corresponding dB number, we use the quotient p_x/p_0 where $p_0 = 2 \times 10^{-5}$ N/m² represents an arbitrarily selected reference value. It is actually the pressure of a sound which one can just detect at the threshold of audibility. The logarithm (base 10) of the ratio p_x/p_0 is multiplied by 20 so that the formula for the noise level L in dB is

$$L = 20 \times \log(p_x/p_0).$$

This seemingly random definition has a number of advantages:

- Instead of using cumbersome powers of ten for pressure, these values are expressed by one, two or three digit numbers.
- The following simple relations hold for the indicated physical units:
- A tenfold increase in sound pressure is expressed as a change of 20 dB.
- If the sound pressure is doubled, we have an increase of $20 \times \log(2) = 20 \times 0.30103 = 6$ dB.
- In the case of a three-fold increase in sound pressure the formula produces a dB change of 9.54, which can be rounded off to 10 dB.
- The energy level of a sound is proportional to the square of the sound pressure, meaning that when the energy is doubled, the decibel level is increased by 3 dB.

Loudness: The noise level of a sound is a purely physical measure, expressed in either N/m² or dB. But this gives no indication of the subjective experience of the loudness of a sound. Sound

waves at different frequencies, exerting the same pressure, are not perceived subjectively as being of equal volume. A sound at a level of 20 dB, having a frequency of 63 Hz, would have to be made about 30 times stronger in order to sound as loud as a 1,000 Hz signal at the same dB level. From the formula already given, that means it would have to be increased by 20 x log(30) = 29.5 dB.

By connecting the points of equal loudness at different frequencies on a dB-Hz diagram, curves known as isophones result. By definition, the measured sound pressure in dB at a frequency of 1,000 Hz is the loudness, expressed using a unit known as the phon. So for example, if one wants to find the 50 phon isophone, a test subject listens to a 1,000 Hz signal having a sound pressure of 50 dB. At all other frequencies the person adjusts a control indicating dB values, until it sounds just as loud as the 1,000 Hz signal. In this way one can plot the dB values corresponding to each of the frequencies to obtain the 50 phon curve. Only at a frequency of 1,000 Hz is the phon scale numerically equal to the decibel scale.

The pressure at which a sound becomes audible is called the threshold of audibility. This corresponds to the 4 phon isophone. If a sound is so loud that it causes pain, the threshold of pain is reached. Its isophone is 130 phon. If our ears were purely mechanical sound detectors, then all isophones would have been horizontal lines.

We are able to distinguish very clearly between the loudness of two sounds. At low sound intensities at a given frequency, a difference of 1 dB is sufficient. At louder levels this difference is even less.

12 orders of magnitude without switching:
The ear has the amazing ability of detecting a range of sound pressure extending over 120 dB. Keeping in mind that 6 dB represents a doubling of sound level, this means that the human ear can handle intensities ranging over 20 powers of 2 (120/6 = 20; 2^{20} = 1,048,576 = approximately one million). In the case of sound energy, doubling occurs every 3 dB because of the physical relationships involved. The human ear thus has

the unique ability of detecting differences in sound energy over a very wide range. The relevant factor is 40 powers of 2 (120/3) which is equal to 12 powers of ten (2^{40} = 1024^4 = 1.099×10^{12}). Expressed differently: The range between the pain threshold and a barely audible sound encompasses an energy ratio of one million million to one. This is an astonishing feat, since it is accomplished with just one range of measurement. No known technical measuring apparatus can do this without switching from one range to another. If, for example, we want to measure voltages in the range from 1 volt to 10,000 volts (4 powers of ten), it can only be done with a single instrument by switching the measuring range.

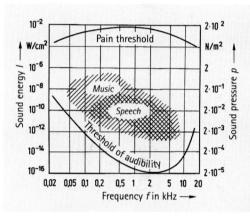

Range of normal human hearing
The threshold of audibility is a curve, meaning that the ear is more sensitive to some frequencies than to others. The optimal range is between 1 kHz and 5 kHz, where sound pressures as low as 2×10^{-5} N/m² can be detected. This is equivalent to an intensity I (sound energy) of 10^{-16} W/cm². The intensity-frequency ranges for speech and music are shaded. The maximum range of hearing lies at about 2 kHz. At this frequency, the range of sound energy we are able to detect spans an almost unimaginable 13 orders of magnitude (powers of ten).

Furthermore, the human ear is an optimally constructed measuring system whose sensitivity reaches the limits of physical possibility. Sound waves are pressure waves having very small

23

amplitudes. The pressure exerted by a barely audible 1,000 Hz tone is 2×10^{-5} N/m². At the same frequency the pain threshold is about six million times greater. The performance of the ear encompasses several powers of ten (Diagram, page 23).

A sound at the threshold of audibility causes the ear drum to vibrate with an amplitude of only 10^{-10} cm. We need to use an extraordinary comparison in order to visualise such a minute displacement. If our body height were increased by a factor of 200 million, it would extend from the earth to the moon. Even at this enormously magnified scale, the ear drum would only vibrate over a distance of 2 mm.

The frequency range of the human ear is approximately 10 octaves. One octave comprises the notes from middle C to C' (or A to A', G to G', etc). This does not imply absolute values, but indicates a doubling of the frequency. Two octaves (e. g. from C to C'') thus range from a given frequency f_1 to a frequency $f_2 = 4 \times f_1$ – a fourfold increase. Similarly three octaves imply an eightfold increase: $f_3 = 2^3 \times f_1$. Human hearing ranges over 10 octaves, from 20 Hz to 20 kHz, involving the factor $2^{10} = 1024 =$ approximately one thousand.

The ability to distinguish between different tones is astonishingly good. Around a frequency of 1,000 Hz we can detect frequency differences as small as 3 Hz or 0.3 %.

a)

b)

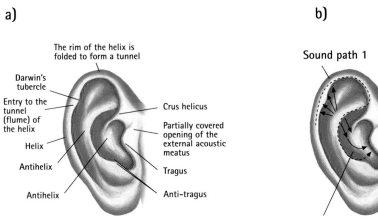

Sound path 1

The rim of the helix is folded to form a tunnel

Darwin's tubercle

Entry to the tunnel (flume) of the helix

Crus helicus

Partially covered opening of the external acoustic meatus

Helix

Antihelix

Tragus

Antihelix

Anti-tragus

Sound path 2

Auricle and sound paths

a) **Auricle:** *Anatomical names of the various parts of the auricle (outer ear) are shown in the illustration above left.*

b) **Possible sound paths:** *Two possible paths, 1 and 2, are indicated in the diagram above right:*
1 shows the route from the antihelix to the acoustic meatus (auditory canal), while route 2 follows the S-shaped curve of the rim of the helix. Route 2 is about 66 mm longer than route 1, so that the time lag is

0.2 milliseconds (0.066 m / 330 m/s = 0.0002 seconds). The result is that the brain has four different sound inputs from the two ears (it's as if there were four ears!): Two of the four are located somewhat higher, and further out, than the other two. The brain receives the same signal at four slightly different instants.

Loudness, duration, and frequency are the properties of a sound which inform us of its character and its origin. But the direction of the sound is also important. The problem of direction finding was solved by the Creator when He endowed us with two ears. To locate the position of a sound source, two factors are involved: the difference in intensity, and the time lag. The ear turned away from a sound source receives the signal a little softer and somewhat later than the other one. The brain can also measure the difference in relative loudness between both ears, and thus estimate the distance of the sound source. Although very small, these time and volume differences are evaluated by the brain in such a way that the direction can be ascertained with some

precision. This measuring process is so accurate that a time lag of 0.00003 seconds between the two ears can be detected clearly. In accoustic orientation terms this means that a sound source located only about 3° from the centre line of the head is recognised as being off-centre.

Measured sound levels: The dB values of various sounds are given in the table below. Sounds louder than 90 dB can cause hearing damage, while a continuous sound of 155 dB can burn the skin. Some sound sources and their dB levels are:

Source	dB
Limit of audibility	15
Rustling of leaves	18

c)

d)

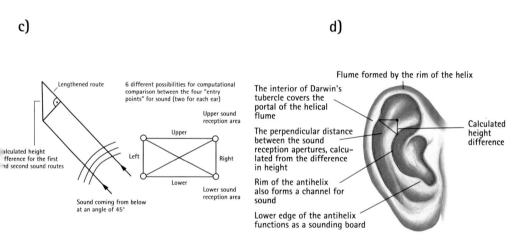

Different computational comparisons of sounds by the brain.

c) Six different values: *As can be seen from the diagram, the four separate locations result in six different sound values to be computed and compared.*

d) Sound reception areas: *The positions of the sound reception areas can be clarified by means of this diagram. If a sound source is located in a direction 45° below one's head, then the sound waves reach the upper reception area along a route which is 9.1 mm longer. The height of the right-angled triangle would then be 13 mm.*

The entry to the tunnel-like rim of the helix is located below Darwin's bulge. The aperture for the shorter route 1 is located where the rim of the antihelix becomes a flume. The sound waves are also reflected into the helix rim by the thickened antihelix from whence it follows the longer route to the ear canal. It could also travel along the shorter route. The shortest link between the two apertures makes an angle of 45°, so that the difference between the two routes is about 18 mm (based on J. Maximilian, E. Irrgang, and B. Andresen).

25

Whispering	25
Spacious office	50
Motor car cruising smoothly	50
Thunder	65
Noisy street traffic	70
Typewriter	70
Waterfall	90
Freight train	98
Sawmill	100
Jet plane (at 600m height)	105
Disco	114
Prop-driven plane starting up	120
Boilermaking	120
Rock concert	125
Pneumatic drill	130
Artillery fire	130
Testing airplane engines	140
Jet engine starting up	145

Let us now consider the structure of the ear.

The auricle: The human auricle, with its attractive relief of ridges, hollows, bulges, curves and grooves, is unmistakeably the same in its basic features, yet is a little different, in each one of us. The fact that these complex and beautiful forms play an important part in the hearing process has only been discovered in recent years.

Sounds are conducted to the external hearing canal along two different paths, with the result that the sound travelling along the shorter route arrives one five thousandth of a second before the other signal. Given that sound travels at a speed of 330 m/s, this means that the difference in path length is about 6.5 cm. This is quite separate from the time difference between the two ears, which enables us to locate the source of various sounds. Such refined accoustic analysis is fairly essential for us. In effect we are able to analyse sounds in three dimensions, in such a way that we can recognise the direction of all incoming sounds, as well as the location and motion of their sources.

Vocal communication requires very accurate identification of the position and movement of someone who is speaking, as well as of all the complex sound sequences involved. Since there are two sound paths for each ear, we virtually possess four ears. This ingenious system is so subtly and cleverly designed, that it all happens without us ever being aware of any doubling or quadrupling of sounds.

Darwin's book, *The Descent of Man and Selection in Relation to Sex* was published in 1871. In it he

The organ of Corti

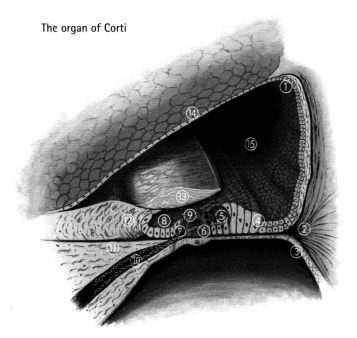

1. Columnar cells
2. Spiral ligament
3. Epithelial cells of the scala tympani
4. Supporting cells (of Hensen)
5. Outer hair cells
6. Interior tunnel
7. Inner hair cells
8. Internal spiral sulcus
9. Pillar cells
10. Cochlear nerve
11. Bony spiral layer
12. Edge of the bony spiral layer
13. Tectorial membrane
14. Vestibular membrane
15. Cochlear duct

denigrated the external human ear, with all its convolutions, as being pointless and useless, a degenerate left-over from some alleged evolutionary history. The little protrusion on the upper outside edge of the auricle has been known since then as "Darwin's tubercle". Generations of researchers after Darwin blindly accepted his verdict on the ear. But in reality, the whole beautiful, convoluted labyrinth that is our auricle is a precise, genetically programmed device which delivers an identical additional signal to the brain after a time lag of one five thousandth of a second (= 0.0002 s, see the diagram on page 24). In effect, one has four ears, two of which are located slightly higher than the other two. The result of this finely tuned system is that the brain is able to process six different values, two of them being the differences between the two upper "ears", two more are those between the two lower "ears", and the third pair is that between the lower "ear" on one side, and the upper "ear" on the other side (see the diagram on page 25). The required computations are carried out at lightning speed in the brain to give us a very sophisticated "sound image" of our surroundings. This structure is also crucial in our astounding ability to voluntarily suppress some sounds to the enhancement of others.

Middle ear: After travelling along the external acoustic meatus, incoming sound waves strike the ear drum, which is set vibrating. The energy transferred in this way is passed on, as the three tiny, connected bones in the middle ear (malleus, incus, and stapes, or hammer, anvil and stirrup) transmit the sound vibrations through the oval window into the inner ear. Weighing only about 10 mg, a tiny percent of the mass of the smallest of coins, these minute bones are the smallest in the entire human body.

The hearing process involves the transfer of air vibrations into the liquid medium of the inner ear. In the normal course of events, the greater part of the sound energy would be reflected at an air/liquid boundary, and such losses would play havoc with the hearing process. To circumvent this, the Creator used a very ingenious interface structure which limits reflection losses to a negligible level.

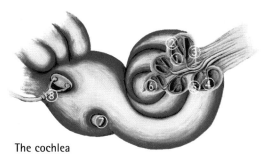

The cochlea

① Scala vestibuli
② Cochlear duct
③ Scala tympani
④ Sensory zone (organ of Corti)
⑤ Vestibular membrane
⑥ Helicotrema
⑦ Round window
⑧ Stapes in oval window

This complex mechanism, comprising the ear drum and the three middle ear bones, exactly matches the sound wave impedance in air to that of the inner ear. The effective vibrational area of the ear drum is about 0.65 cm², which is 20 times that of the oval window (only 0.032 cm²). This is equivalent to an amplification factor of 20. In addition, the leverage afforded by the malleus-incus-stapes linkup provides a further amplification factor of 3.

Inner ear: It is clear that a massive amplification factor is involved in the conversion of air waves (at the ear drum) to the vibrations of the liquid in the cochlea. The inner ear, comprising both the balance organ and the cochlea (Latin *cóchlea* = snail), is housed in the solid bone of the skull. A second conversion takes place here; mechanical vibrations are changed into electric neural (nerve) impulses.

The cochlear duct is filled with a highly viscous liquid (Latin *viscum* = birdlime, sticky, or thick), called the endolymph. There are two more liquid-filled spaces on either side, the scala vestibuli (Latin *scala* = steps; *vestibuli* = forecourt), and the scala tympani (Latin *tympanum* = drum). Both of these cavities are filled with a somewhat

27

less viscous liquid, called the perilymph, and they are connected at the apex of the cochlea (by the helicotrema). The scala vestibuli begins at the oval window, and the scala tympani ends at the membrane of the round window.

The cochlear duct and the scala vestibuli are separated by an elastic sheet, called the vestibular membrane. This membrane reproduces the wave-shaped changes in volume caused by the incident sound. The endolymph then transmits the vibrations to the basilar membrane which lies between the cochlear duct and the scala tympani. Eventually the round window is reached via the perilymph. Because of this shortcut the vibrations do not have to travel all the way round through the helicotrema. The vestibular and basilar membranes thus vibrate in unison.

The spiral-shaped bulge of the organ of Corti is located above the basilar membrane. It consists of sensory cells, twelve thousand of which, arranged in rows of three to five, make up the exterior hair cells. The interior 3,500 hair cells as well as the structural support cells lie in one row. The 12,000 sensory cells are arranged on a 32 mm long lamina in four parallel rows having a total width of only 1/20 mm. Their geometrical sequence and distribution resemble that of piano keys in a linear scale. At one end the cells are tuned to a maximum frequency of between 10 and 20 kHz, which descends to about 30 Hz at the other end.

When sounds are received, the basilar membrane vibrates in sympathy, but the amplitude is inconceivably minute, only about 10^{-11} m. This is equal to 100 picometres or one thousand millionth of a cm (one million million pm = 1 metre) which approaches the size of a few atoms. The tips of the outer hair cells penetrate a covering membrane (the tectorial membrane) which projects into the cochlear duct. Volume changes in this passage cause the basilar membrane to move relative to the tectorial membrane so that the sensory hairs experience a slight shearing pressure. These stimuli are then transmitted as electrical signals along the cochlear (auditory) nerve to the brain. It should be noted that these signals not

only travel to the brain, but also in the reverse direction. For this purpose there are two types of neural tissue at the base of the hair cells, namely the afferent (leading to the brain) and the efferent fibres leading to the hair cells. The reason for this feedback is not yet understood and this is only one of the many unsolved puzzles.

There are about 15,000 receptor cells (hair cells) in the cochlea and they are sensitive to different sound frequencies (Diagram, page 27). The hair cells are located in ordered rows on the basilar membrane, which is a thin wall extending through the entire cochlea, following all its convolutions. An incident sound image is separated into its single component frequencies, each of which stimulates only a small fraction of the 15,000 sensory cells located at a specific position on the basilar membrane. The functioning of the cochlea is highly complex, and its ingenious structure is not yet fully understood.

Special abilities of the ear: The ear is the most sensitive human sensory organ. Sounds with frequencies between about 20 Hz and 16 kHz are audible. Lower frequencies are felt rather than heard. All natural sounds are highly complex; pure tones consisting of a single sinusoidal frequency are not found in nature. But when they are produced artificially, they are of great experimental use. Sounds and noises can be considered as a mixture of sinusoidal tones having different frequencies and amplitudes. A tone can be regarded as being the elementary unit for natural sounds and noises. A 3 kHz note having an energy level of only 4×10^{-17} W/cm^2 can be heard, and in general audible sound intensities lie in the range between 10^{-16} and 10^{-4} W/cm^2 (Diagram, page 23).

Speech detection: Amongst all living things the gift of speech is unique. Only man has been endowed by the Creator with this exceptional means of communication. It essentially requires four independent organ systems:

- The larynx which produces the sounds (phonation).
- The mouth and throat which modulate the sounds produced by the larynx to form recog-

nisable vowels and consonants. This process is called articulation.

- The brain's motor speech centre controls both the above processes.
- Hearing is essential for the continuous feedback control which orderly speech requires; hearing ourselves as we speak, the so-called aural-vocal cycle. This cycle depends on the intact physiological operation of all the auditory mechanisms and pathways leading to perception of speech in the brain's sensory speech centre. It also involves the psyche and the intellect. It should be obvious that the ear is much more than a technologically sophisticated physical detection device. It is in fact an integral component of a system involving the transmission of meaningful information, of thoughts, ideas, and intelligence, and the beauty of music.

Origin of the ear: From whence does the ingenious construction of the ear (and the eye) derive? The Psalmist gives a concise and striking answer: "Does he who implanted the ear, not hear? Does he who formed the eye, not see?" (Ps 94:9). This is also affirmed in Proverbs 20:12: "Ears that hear and eyes that see – the LORD has made them both." The ear did not originate in some evolutionary process, but it was made by the almighty Creator. Jesus calls those people blessed who hear the Word of God (Matt 13:16) and He urges the bystanders to listen: "He who has ears, let him hear" (e. g. Matt 11:15, Matt 13:9,43). All the messages which the resurrected and ascended Lord Jesus Christ sent to the seven churches end with the admonishment "He who has an ear, let him hear..." (Rev 2:7,11,17,29; Rev 3:6,13,22). The Creator blessed us with ears which are indispensable organs for the reception and processing of accoustic information in this life, and He desires that His Word should be given its proper place.

The sense of smell

– beyond words

From earliest childhood, we are accompanied by scents and smells. We store the experience of them in such a way that we can recognise them with certainty, even decades later. Many smells remind us of specific experiences – like the fragrances of spring, the scent of cedar trees or violets, the freshness of a forest after a summer downpour, the lightly salty tang of sea air, the unmistakeable aroma of freshly unearthed potatoes, or a roast turkey at Christmas time. Unpleasant odours also leave lasting impressions, for example hot tar on a road surface, a damp musty cellar, rotten eggs, or even the putrid smell of a decaying cadaver. Long forgotten scents, even after lying hidden under the accumulated experiences of many passing years, can suddenly burst into our recollection. The nose is an indispensable organ, with which we perceive many, many details of our surroundings.

Smelling and tasting are chemical senses. Without our olfactory sense we would only be able to taste sweet, salty, bitter, and sour. It is the nose that makes eating and drinking pleasurable. Through our nose we can detect danger, and also enjoy the fragrances of flowers, spices and perfumes.

Structure and function of the nose: The fan-shaped fibres of the olfactory nerve occupy an appreciable volume of the complex human nasal structure. Odour molecules collide with specific receptor molecules, fitting together like a lock and key. There are between 10 and 25 million receptor cells in the olfactory region which covers an area of about 2.5 cm^2 on each side. These receptors are part of the nervous system and are known as olfactory neurons. Like the taste cells, they are supported by basal cells and are continually renewed, their half-life being about ten days. The olfactory cells measure only about 5 to 15 µm (1 µm = one thousandth of a millimetre). Molecules which cause odours are captured by the receptors in the mucous membrane of the nose. The olfactory information is then converted into electrical impulses which are transmitted to the so-called olfactory bulb which distributes them in the brain.

We can distinguish far more than 10,000 different scents. This wide range can be extended even further with practice; professional perfume testers, and coffee and wine tasters excel in this ability. Only substances that are sufficiently volatile to emit minute particles into the air can be smelled. This multitude of odours exceeds the capacity of our vocabulary to describe them all.

The nose is also essential for respiration. Since the lungs prefer damp, warm, clear air, air is moistened and warmed by its long passage over the mucous membranes of the nose. Most of the coarser, harmful particles in air are trapped by the nose's fine hairs or its thick secretions (mucus).

The olfactory mucous membrane is located fairly deep inside the nose. It contains millions of receptor cells embedded in elongated supporting cells. These sensory nerve cells are stimulated by odours and also transmit the olfactory messages directly to the brain. They are "direct intermediaries" between the outside world and the brain. From each of their ends, a tuft of fine hairlike projections called cilia (Latin *cilium* = eyelash) extends into the olfactory mucous membrane, in which the molecules that cause odours are dissolved, having found their way through the nasal cavity. These olfactory nerve cells are continuously renewed from basal neuronal (stem) cells. This is somewhat exceptional, since many nerve cells of humans and other organisms are not replaced when they die.

It has recently been discovered that the number of detectable odours is directly proportional to the number of genes. In the case of human beings (and mammals generally) there are about 1,000 genes which code for the same number of different olfactory receptors, each of which occurs in thousands of the millions of sensory cells. If a mammal has 100,000 genes, then this means around one percent of them code for proteins which can bind with odour-causing molecules. This is the largest group of related genes discovered so far. It is therefore difficult to measure various odours objectively, since every person, apart from identical twins, has his/her own genetically determined olfactory preferences.

This contrasts sharply with the small number of optical receptor pigments in the eye. Only three types of pigments are required to distinguish between thousands of shades of colour, because the principle of recognition is fundamentally different: All three types can receive a wide range of partially overlapping wave lengths of light, each being most sensitive in a different part of the optical spectrum. The brain finally combines and compares the optical stimuli. Olfactory signals cannot be handled in a similar way, because a large number of qualitatively widely different chemical components would have to be compared.

The process used by the brain to decode olfactory information is one of the central and most difficult unsolved problems in neuro-physiology.

The indescribable sense: The sense of smell truly is the sense beyond words. It can be extraordinarily exact, but it is practically impossible to describe a scent to somebody who hasn't experienced it personally. We move about 12 cubic metres (12 m³) of air per day by breathing in and out 12,000 times. Inhalation requires about 2 seconds, and exhalation 5 seconds. During this time odour molecules also move with the airflow. We can describe something we have seen in the finest detail, using plenty of images so that the listener can get a clear picture of our experience. But in the case of odours, we can only express general feelings like pleasant, horrible, wonderful, or exciting. Just try to describe in words the fragrance of your marriage partner, of a shoe shop, a bakery, or an old library! Our memory for odours is astounding – nothing can stir up old memories better than a certain scent.

The scientifically incomprehensible sense:

Most smells are a mixture of a large number of odour-causing substances. Wine, for example, contains about 200 and coffee about 500 different ones. It has up to now not been possible to reduce the multiplicity of scents to mixtures of a few primary odours. The phenomenon of smell is still poorly understood scientifically.

Our olfactory sense is extremely sensitive and exceeds the capabilities of most technological measuring instruments. The threshold of detection for ethyl mercaptan is about 10^{-13} g (one ten million millionth of a gram = 10^9 molecules). It is not clear why many molecules which are chemically quite different have the same olfactory effect. On the other hand, very similar chemical compounds can smell completely different. D-carvone smells like cumin, while L-carvone has a mint-like smell. But both have exactly the same chemical formula, except that the former is right-handed and the latter has a left-handed structure. Like your two hands, these are identical, but mirror images of each other (stereoisomers).

Everybody has his/her own very specific personal scent, which is just as unique as a fingerprint. A baby recognises its mother by smell, and adults can distinguish between male and female. Dogs readily identify individuals by their odour and can even recognise their owner in the case of identical twins. A border collie has about 220 million olfactory cells. As far as humans are concerned, the following traces of odour-causing substance per liter of air are detectable:

0.000 000 004	g acetone
0.000 000 0012	g phenol
0.000 000 004	g naphthalene
0.000 000 000 016	g camphor
0.000 000 000 041	g nitrobenzol
0.000 000 000 005	g vanillin
0.000 000 000 0004	g skatol

Perfumes can be beneficial for health (French *parfum* = pleasant scent): Perfumes began their triumphal progress as incense in Mesopotamia. The word "perfume" is derived from the Latin *per* = by or through, and *fumus* = odour. The first country known to have used perfumes regularly and extravagantly was Egypt. Their pompous burial and embalming rites required spices and ointments. In the time of Queen Hatsheput (1490 – 1468 BC) perfume became a common passion. Cleopatra (69 – 30 BC) was also a fervent lover of perfume. The cedarwood boat on which she received Anthony had perfumed sails. Incense containers surrounded her throne, and she herself was perfumed from head to toe. The buildings of the kings of antiquity were filled with scents. They preferred cedarwood for constructing their palaces, because of its sweet resinous smell, as well as its ability to repel insects.

The Bible and perfumes: Aromatic substances also play a significant role in the Bible. A mixture of flowers, aromatic seeds and fruit, and olive oil, is described as "precious oil" in Psalm 133:2, and in Esther 2:12 we read of "six months with oil of myrrh and six with perfumes and cosmetics". Aromatic plants and spices are mentioned many times in the Bible: aloe, balm, galbanum, henna, nard, sweet sedge, cinnamon, and myrrh. Aloes (Numbers 24:6, Psalm 45:8, Song of Songs 4:14) were used for preparing Jesus' body for burial (John 19:39). In Solomon's Song of Songs very many scents, fragrances, perfumes, and ointments are mentioned. A certain American lady author described this portion of the Old Testament as the most perfumed poem of all times and as a sensual love story saturated with perfumes and ointments. Love is described in terms of fragrant scents: "How delightful is your love ... How much more pleasing is your love than wine, and the fragrance of your perfume than any spice! ... The fragrance of your garments is like that of Lebanon" (Song of Songs 4:10-11). Nard is an aromatic and very costly plant listed among fragrant flowers and spices in Song of Songs 4:13-14. The perfume used to anoint Jesus in Bethany, contained nard (Mark 14:3, John 12:3). According to John 12:5 this perfume was so expensive that its price was equivalent to a year's wages (300 silver denarii). The gifts brought to Jesus by the wise men from the east, comprised incense, myrrh and gold (Matthew 2:11).

The phrase "A pleasing aroma to the LORD" is used frequently in the Old Testament (e. g. Gen 8:21, Ex 29:18,25,41, Lev 1:9,13,7). This means that God is pleased with those deeds. When Noah built an altar and sacrificed burnt offerings, "the LORD smelled the pleasing aroma ..." (Gen 8:21). God Himself can smell. He gave us this sense to enrich our lives and to be like Him also in this respect.

Perfumes are also employed in another biblical parable (2 Cor 2:14-16). The triumphal entry of Roman generals was accompanied by prisoners who carried jars of incense so that everybody could smell these perfumes expressing the victory. In the same way everybody who lives in Christ should spread the fragrance of victory. Paul wrote to the Corinthians: "For we are to God the aroma of Christ among those who are being saved and those who are perishing. To the one we are the smell of death; to the other, the fragrance of life" (2 Cor 2:15-16).

This gospel message blows over its hearers like an aromatic cloud, but its effect can vary greatly. Some of them accept the words which then become a blessing – it is for them a fragrance of life which engenders everlasting life. For the indifferent and for those who reject the message proclaimed, it becomes a deadly odour like a poisonous fog bearing the putrid smell of decaying bodies, a harbinger of death, of eternal perdition. Only a hair's breadth separates salvation and doom.

Quote:

Richard Axel, professor of biochemistry and molecular biophysics at the University of Columbia, New York:

"Till now science has only been groping in the dark in trying to discover the rules governing the way our olfactory sense can unlock the immeasurable structure of our memories."

The sense of taste

– not just for connoisseurs

Our taste sense functions only on contact. The taste buds are located in the mouth, mostly on the tongue. There are only four basic tastes: sweet, sour, salt, and bitter. It is remarkable that all the various tastes we can think of, arise from a combination of these four. We are able to distinguish between the most delicate of gastronomic nuances, as is regularly done by professional tasters of wine, coffee, tea, and cheese. But note that the sense of smell also plays an important role.

Everyday language seems to regard the palate as having something to do with the sensation of taste. We might refer to an exceptional meal as having 'tickled the palate', or speak of a connoisseur as 'having a fine palate'. But taste is actually located on the tongue, which can be divided into four zones, each primarily sensitive to one of the four basic tastes. The front of the tongue is mostly sensitive to sweetness, whereas bitter is perceived more to the rear. The edges of the tongue are more sensitive to sour towards the rear, and to salty substances towards the tip.

The difference between sweet and sour is so important that it finds expression in idiomatic language. A child, a girl friend, or a kitten, are all described as sweet. On the other hand defeat, pain, or a disappointment are perceived as bitter. When we have to bear a heavy load, we speak of a "bitter pill".

We can only smell something when it starts to evaporate; in the same way we can only taste something if it can be dissolved in water. Other senses are involved in how we experience the taste of something. First, the sense of smell (the aroma of the food), then our general chemical sense (its pungency or "hotness", like chili peppers). Also, our somato-visceral sense (Greek soma = body, Latin viscera = intestines, inner organs) which communicates something of the temperature, structure and consistency of food. The important role of our olfactory sense in enjoying a meal becomes obvious when we have a clogged nose. Odours are much more readily detected than flavours: for example, we require 25,000 times as many molecules to taste a cherry tart than to smell it.

The actual tasting is done by the taste buds, of which there are between 5,000 and 10,000 in the papillae on our tongues. A papilla is about 70 μm high and has a diameter of 40 μm. It is not possible to definitively correlate the taste of a substance with its chemical properties. Different sugars (like saccharose, fructose, maltose and glucose) all taste sweet, but so do lead salts.

Our high sensitivity for bitter substances like the alkaloids (quinine, caffeine, morphine, nicotine, and strychnine) is noteworthy. Such substances are often toxic, so our sense of taste provides a vital warning.

We have been given our sense of taste for testing and also enjoying our food. It also has an effect on digestion, by influencing the quantity and type of the secretions of the digestive (especially salivary) glands.

Certain substances can be tasted even when greatly diluted, and some thresholds are given below. Dissolved in one cc of liquid, we can still taste:

0.000 001 g	saccharine	(sweet)
0.000 004 g	quinine	(bitter)
0.000 05 g	caffeine	(bitter)
0.000 01 g	hydrochloric acid	(sour)
0.001 g	table salt	(salty)

The general chemical sense: In addition to smell and taste, we also have a third chemical sense: the general chemical sense. The receptors involved are free nerve endings located in the mucous membranes of the eyes, mouth, throat, and nose. They react to irritants as well as to the same chemicals which give rise to odours and tastes, if these are present in relatively high concentrations. We can experience a burning sensation (e. g. in the eyes when peeling onions, in the mouth and throat when eating something "hot and spicy"), or a stinging (in the nose when cutting an onion). We are not really aware of it being an independent sense in its own right, but its purpose is to protect us from dangerous substances. There are several responses which lessen the irritation, like the secretion of tears, mucus, or saliva, or simply closing our eyes.

Flavours mentioned in the Bible: According to Job 12:11 our sense organs have a proving or testing function: "Does not the ear test words as the tongue tastes food?" The goodness of God can be observed by our senses, as written in Psalm 34:8: "Taste and see that the LORD is good." In 1 Peter 2:2-3 we read that recently redeemed persons need spiritual milk to grow in faith, "so that by it you may grow up in your salvation, now that you have tasted that the Lord is good."

In parables Jesus always described the essence of heaven in terms of a great festival or banquet. He mentions a wedding feast: "The kingdom of heaven is like a king who prepared a wedding banquet for his son" (Matt 22:2), and: "A certain man (meaning God) was preparing a great banquet (the festival of heaven) and invited many guests" (Luke 14:16). Some of the invited guests made excuses with serious consequences. They missed entry into heaven: "I tell you, not one of those men who were invited, will get a taste of my banquet" (Luke 14:24). The joys of heaven are described in terms of taste. In Luke 12:37 Jesus asserts that He Him-

Muscles of the tongue

① External acoustic meatus
② Styloid process
③ Styloglossus muscle
④ Hyoglossus muscle
⑤ Hyoid bone
⑥ Genioglossus muscle
⑦ Lower jaw (mandible)
⑧ Tongue
⑨ Incisor tooth
⑩ Palatoglossus muscle

self will serve believers as his guests in heaven: "He will dress himself to serve, will have them recline at the table, and will come and wait on them."

In the Bible tasting is often employed as a metaphor for both intense enjoyment and suffering. He who lives a life dedicated to God, tastes His goodness (Ps 34:9, 1 Peter 2:3), and we read in Hebrews 6:4-5 of those "who have *tasted* the heavenly gift ... who have *tasted* the goodness of the Word of God, and the powers of the coming age."

Jesus "suffered death, so that by the grace of God he might taste death for everyone" (Hebr 2:9). This means much more than bodily death. By his death He paid the wages of sin (Rom 6:23), He suffered in our place the judgement that would have come upon us if we had no Saviour. His assertion is valid for everybody who believes in Him, namely: "I tell you the truth, if a man keeps my word, he will never see death" (John 8:51, or "taste death" as written in verse 52).

Since the essence of eternity is described in verbs dealing with our sense organs, we might also put it like this: Eternity is a place of everlasting observation through our senses.

Quote:

French proverb: "When you put a tasty morsel in your mouth, you send a message of joy to your heart."

Section of a taste papilla
(papilla vallata). An enlarged section appears alongside.

Section of a single taste bud.

① Columnar cells
② Moat
③ Taste papilla
④ Taste bud
⑤ Hair-like structures (microvilli) protrude into the moat.
⑥ Epithelium of the tongue
⑦ Sensory taste cells
⑧ Structural cell
⑨ Nerve fibres
⑩ Salivary glands

37

The sense of touch

– it's all over the skin

We become aware of the versatility of our tactile sense when we think of such diverse experiences as caressing, fondling, itching, nibbling, tickling, scratching, and kissing. Or consider some special situations like jumping into a cold pool on a hot summer day, withdrawing your foot from a muddy patch, or the crunching of wet sand between your toes. People who are deaf and blind demonstrate that it is possible to orientate themselves by their sense of touch. If we had no tactile sense, it would have been like living in vague, dull surroundings where one could lose a leg or burn one's skin, or get disorientated without even noticing it.

There are many metaphors in our language which refer to touching and feeling. Our emotions are called feelings, and when we are moved, we say that something has *touched* us. Problems can be "ticklish" or "tough". Some people have to be handled "with kid gloves". Music teachers chide their pupils for not having enough "feeling in their fingertips", meaning that a difficult-to-describe "something" is lacking in their performance.

The physiological term for the transmission of information by means of receptors (Latin *receptor* = recorder) is sensibility (Latin *sensibilis* = observable). A receptor is the end of a nerve fibre, or a specialised cell, which can detect stimuli and convert them into neural impulses.

General sensibility: Tremendous amounts of information are detected by receptors and are subsequently processed in the central nervous system. This complex process is known as sensibility. The receptors are located in the skin, in structures like muscles and skeletal joints, or in internal organs, and are respectively known as superficial, deep, and visceral sensibility (Latin *viscera* = intestine). As distinct from the other four senses (hearing, seeing, smelling and tasting), these three types are known collectively as somato-visceral sensibility. Only a small fraction of all these signals are consciously perceived. Several kinds of receptors can be distinguished according to the stimuli which they detect, namely mechanical, thermal, chemical, osmotic, and polymodal receptors. The latter refer to more than one type of stimulus.

Sensibility of the skin: We will here restrict ourselves to superficial sensibility, namely the perceptions mediated by the skin *(cutis)*. This is a (nearly) watertight covering which protects all body tissues from physical damage. At the same time the skin is a highly sensitive sense organ which can simultaneously detect various stimuli that can be quite independent of one another. A large number of different sensations can be perceived via the skin: the softness of a cat's fur, the roughness of a masonry wall, the smoothness of ice, the pleasant warm sensation of a sauna, but also the thorns of a rosebush, or the burning pain of a fresh wound. Strong emotions can be aroused through the skin, as by a passionate kiss or tender caresses. Many properties of objects cannot be appraised by hearing, seeing, or smelling, but only by touch, as for example, weight, temperature, hardness, roughness, dampness, stickiness, and elasticity. We recognise surface structures and shapes by touch.

There are very many sensitive points in the skin, but they are not evenly distributed. They are closer together on face and hands than, for example, on the back, which is therefore less sensitive. There are three independent skin senses, namely touch, temperature, and pain.

Not only do we have unique fingerprints, the patterns of our skin pores are also unique. The skin is a dual-layered membrane. The inner, spongy, leathery layer has a thickness of between one and two millimetres. It consists essentially of connective tissue which is rich in the protein collagen. It protects and cushions the body, and it contains hair follicles, nerve ends, and sweat-

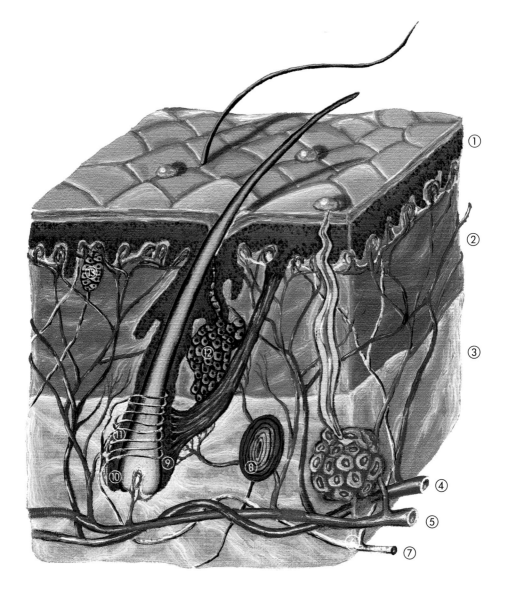

A section of human skin.
The layers of the epidermis, the dermis, and the inner skin are clearly visible.

① Epidermis
② Dermis
③ Subcutaneous layer
④ Vein
⑤ Artery
⑥ Sweat gland
⑦ Nerve
⑧ Pacinian (Vater's) corpuscle (pressure sensitive receptor)
⑨ Hair muscle (erector pili)
⑩ Internal root sheath
⑪ Nerve sheath around hair root
⑫ Sebaceous gland
⑬ Meissner's corpuscle (touch sensitive receptor)

glands, as well as blood capillaries and lymphatic vessels. In contrast, the thickness of the outer layer, the epidermis (Greek *epi* = upon, above; *derma* = skin), is only between 0.07 and 0.12 mm.

Our skin separates our bodies from the outside world. It encloses us, gives us our individual shapes, protects us from intruders, cools or warms us, and conserves our body liquids. Surprisingly, it contributes about one sixth of our body weight, although the epidermis itself weighs only about 500 g. The total area of the skin amounts to approximately 1.6 square metres. It is watertight, washable, and elastic. The skin is thickest on the palms of our hands and on the soles of our feet, and thinnest in the armpits and on the eyelids.

Our skin – by numbers: One square centimetre of skin contains:

6,000,000	cells
100	sweat glands
15	sebaceous glands
5,000	sensory corpuscles
200	pain points (receptor areas)
25	pressure points
12	cold-sensitive points
2	heat-sensitive points

The most important property of the skin is that it contains our sense of touch, which is located in the dermal layer. The outer layer is insensitive, rubs off easily, and causes the ring left in the bath after bathing.

The sense of touch is difficult to investigate. All the other senses have a definite key organ which can be studied, but the skin is spread over the entire body and cannot easily be delimited or "switched off". In the case of vision, scientists can observe blind persons to learn more about seeing, and they can study deaf people to learn more about hearing. But this is impossible for the sense of touch.

Touching is ten times as strong as verbal or emotional contact. If touching were not pleasant,

living things would not procreate. If we did not enjoy touching and caressing, there would be no sex.

A foetus feels the moist warmth inside the womb; it perceives the heartbeats and the internal rhythms of its mother. The sense of touch is the first sense to develop. It functions automatically, before the newborn baby's eyes even open to observe the world.

It has been discovered that there are many more kinds of receptors than the four basic ones through which we experience warmth, coldness, pain, and pressure. All the different tactile sensations are more complex than these four, and they cause us to respond variously.

Tactile experiences (Latin *tactilis* = touchable): Mechanical stimuli cause several different sensations: stroking, touching, vibration, pressure, and tension. The fingertips and the tip of the tongue are especially sensitive. The fingertips can feel a sharp point if the impression is only 10 µm, and in the case of a vibrating stimulus pressed into the skin, can feel it even if this is less than 1 µm.

Other functions of the skin: In addition to its important function as a tactile sense organ, there are several others, of which only a few are mentioned below:

1 The skin protects passively, as well as actively, against injurious external influences. It can destroy invading infective agents.

2 The skin plays an important role in controlling the temperature of the body, which should not deviate from 37° C because most organs function optimally at this temperature. Heat loss can be increased or reduced by increasing or reducing the flow of blood through the skin's network of small blood vessels. About three quarters of the heat loss is effected by radiation and conduction. The other quarter is effected by the evaporation of water, partly unnoticed through the skin and the lungs, and partly by perspiration. The invisible evaporation through the skin comprises one third of the total dermal loss of water.

3 In addition to sweat, the skin also secretes sebum, an oily substance which lubricates the hairs and the epidermis. Sweat-glands are exceptionally numerous on the hands and the soles of the feet. There are about 200 million sweat-glands which secrete approximately one litre of water per day through orifices in the skin.

4 The skin also performs a respiratory function, handling between one and two percent of the total gas exchange of the body. It absorbs oxygen, and carbon dioxide can pass through it in both directions.

5 Pain acts as a guardian of our health. It is usually invoked indirectly by pain mediating chemicals accumulating in body tissues, which then stimulate free nerve endings.

The Bible and the sense of touch: God has all the senses which we have. Since we are made in His image, He blessed us with our various senses. King Belshazzar was told that he had set himself up against the Lord of heaven, because he "praised the gods of silver and gold, of bronze, iron, wood and stone, which cannot see or hear or understand" (in the German translation "understand" is rendered as "*feel*", Daniel 5:23). Man-made idols are characterised as having no sense organs. In contrast, the living God can *see, hear*, and *feel*. The risen Christ wasn't an imaginary figure, but He was so real that He could be seen, heard, and touched. When Jesus appeared suddenly amongst his disciples, they were frightened, because they thought that they were seeing a ghost. To convince them that He was genuine and real, He allowed them to touch Him: "Look at my hands and my feet. It is I myself! *Touch* me and see; a ghost does not have flesh and bones, as you see I have" (Luke 24:39).

John begins his first epistle by testifying that he has observed the Son of God by means of his own senses. He is an eye-witness as well as an aural and a tactile witness of Jesus: "That which was from the beginning, which we have heard, which we have seen with our eyes, which we have looked at and our hands have *touched* – this we proclaim concerning the Word of life... We proclaim to you what we have seen and heard ..." (1 John 1:1,3).

Our sense organs

– in this world and the next

The quality of our lives is determined to a great extent by our senses. We take them for granted, only thinking about them when they stop working in the way we're used to. Just having a clogged nose makes a big difference to the flavour of our favourite dish. Permanent impairments of one sort or another may force us to wear glasses or use a hearing aid. If a sense we have been used to all our life is lost completely, it can be terrible and frightening, because our senses, with all their possibilities and limitations, are so closely interwoven with the central 'I', with our innermost being.

The sense organs of our **present** body cease to function at death. But is it the end; the real and final end? The Bible answers this question with a resounding NO! God created us as eternal beings whose existence will never end. In Luke 16 Jesus tells of two people whose earthly existence ended with their death, but both of them had all their senses in the next world [1].

One of them was a rich man with only one purpose, namely to gather riches and fine clothes and to enjoy the pleasantries of life. He ignored God completely. His name is not even mentioned, although many people looked up to him and envied him his possessions and his influence. His idea of life is similar to that of many of our contemporaries, who also strive towards riches, power and honour and accept these as their due.

The name of the other person, Lazarus, is mentioned by Jesus. He was poor, undernourished, and not esteemed by his fellows, but he knew

[1] Note: Luke 16:19-31 is often erroneously regarded as a parable, but in contrast to the known parables, there is no indication that it is one. Furthermore, the names of actual persons are used (Lazarus, Abraham, Moses). This is a clear indication that it is not a parable.

that God cared for him, because he had a living relationship with God.

Jesus describes their situations after their death: "The time came when the beggar died and the angels carried him to Abraham's side. The rich man also died and was buried. In hell, where he was in torment, he looked up ..." (Luke 16:22-23). Both of them died and have left this earth; now they find themselves in completely different places. Although they lived in the same city, their present abodes are fundamentally different. One person lives in glory, and the other in torment.

Life does not end with biological death. On the contrary, our existence with all our faculties never ends, since we are eternal creatures. This is a true fact, whether we believe it or not. We were born without our permission. We will all die without our permission. And we will exist for ever whether we believe it or not; nobody will ask what our preferences are in this regard. We experience the certainty of eternity in our innermost being, since God has placed this knowledge in our hearts (Eccl 3:11).

On the day of resurrection our earthly body will be changed into an everlasting one: "The body that is sown, is perishable, it is raised imperishable... It is sown a natural body, it is raised a spiritual body. If there is a natural body, there is also a spiritual body" (1 Cor 15:42-44). The spiritual body is imperishable, it is eternal, and it has all the sensory inputs and experiences of consciousness. The Bible mentions two completely different locations for our eternal residence, namely heaven and hell. The former is a glorious life with God, and in the other we will be estranged for ever from God in the place of damnation.

Both heaven and hell are places where our senses function, places of conscious experience. This is now discussed in terms of biblical affirmations:

45

Heaven:

a) *Heaven is a place where we will see and hear:* In the first place we will see God the Father and Jesus in person: "we shall be like him, for we shall see him (Jesus) as he is" (1 John 3:2). Furthermore: "No eye has seen, no ear has heard, no mind has conceived what God has prepared for those who love Him" (1 Cor 2:9). Here on earth we are astounded by God's providence and wisdom; how much more will we be astonished when we see Him face-to-face in heaven, and enjoy his presence eternally!

b) *Heaven is a place where we will taste and smell*: The essence of heaven is described in the New Testament as a great banquet where there will be feasting. At the last supper Jesus told his disciples "I will not drink of this fruit of the vine from now on until that day when I drink it anew with you in my Father's kingdom" (Matt 26:29). Also in the parable of the royal banquet where the essence of heaven with God as Host is described, we read: "I have prepared my dinner" (Matt 22:4). In Luke 12:37 we find another equally important statement in this regard: "He will dress himself to serve, will have them recline at the table, and will come and wait on them." If the Son of God invites us to dinner, we may presume that the spread will be exceedingly rich and excellent.

c) *Heaven is a place full of wonderful experiences*: When the prodigal son returned to his father, he prepared a feast for him. After everything was ready, we read in Luke 15:24: "So they began to celebrate." Another very important aspect of heaven has now been expressed, namely that it is a place of indescribable and everlasting joy. Everything which pleases us will be richly available in heaven – love, peace, friendship, and well-being.

It is noteworthy that Jesus addresses all five senses during His last supper. In this way He reminds us of our salvation which He effected, and consequently also of heaven:

When the Lord's supper is celebrated, the words for its institution (1 Cor 11:23 ff) are usually read. This involves the sense of hearing.

The bread and the wine are firstly observed visually, then we see them as signs of the Lord's presence.
We accept the bread, using our sense of touch. "Taste and see that the Lord is good" (Ps 34:8). When we eat and drink, our senses of tasting and smelling are also involved.

Hell:

a) *Hell is a place of thirst and torment*: The rich man in Luke 16 calls to Abraham: "Have pity on me and send Lazarus to dip the tip of his finger in water and cool my tongue, because I am in agony in this fire" (Luke 16:24). In contrast, Jesus says: "He who comes to Me, will never go hungry, and he who believes in Me, will never be thirsty" (John 6:35).

b) *Hell is a place for remembering*: The knowledge of this life does not vanish when we die. In the place of damnation the rich man thinks of his brothers who lived just as godlessly as he did. He realises that he could do nothing for them, and thus requests Abraham to send Lazarus to them: "Then I beg you, father, send Lazarus to my father's house, for I have five brothers. Let him warn them, so that they will not also come to this place of torment." Abraham replied: "They have Moses and the Prophets; let them listen to them" (Luke 16:27-29). It is a fact that nobody returns from death to warn his relatives. Our only guide to salvation is the Word of God – the Bible!

c) *Hell is a place of darkness*: In this life we enjoy very many wonderful sensations through our eyes and our ears. 83,000 people were present at the colourful opening ceremony of the centennial Olympics in Atlanta on the 19th of July 1996, and 3,500 million people all over the world watched the four hour show on TV. About 5,500 technicians and others cooperated to produce this magnificent opera-like sound-and-light presentation. Why were the spectators prepared to travel so far and to pay hundreds of dollars for an admission ticket? They wanted to see, hear and experience something special. In the same way heaven can be regarded as an immeasurably superior "presentation" of beautiful and glorious

46

experiences, with the added and indescribable bonus of having no time limits. By contrast, hell is a place of darkness, offering no positive experiences for eye and ear. In the parable of the talents Jesus says: "And throw that worthless servant outside, into the darkness, where there will be weeping and gnashing of teeth" (Matt 25:30).

When reading the Bible, it is noteworthy that nobody preached so incisively, so fully, and so often about hell, as Jesus. Why did He do that, seeing that nobody else has ever loved people so much as He? It is precisely because of His love that He warned against this real place: "If your right eye causes you to sin, gouge it out and throw it away. It is better for you to lose one part of your body than for your whole body to be thrown in hell" (Matt 5:29). With these words of the Sermon on the Mount Jesus warns us with the utmost urgency to make sure that we do not end up in that place. We perceive the same extreme urgency in Matthew 18:8: "If your hand or your foot causes you to sin, cut it off and throw it away. It is better for you to enter life maimed or crippled, than to have two hands or two feet and be thrown into eternal fire."

These words of warning from the mouth of Christ have essentially helped to determine the purpose of this book. It is our wish that as many people as possible will be saved from hell and won for heaven. The practical details for achieving this are explained in the second part of this book.

The heart

– more than a high-tech pump

Did you know that the human heart beats 100,000 times a day? This amounts to 2,500 million times over 70 years, pumping enough blood to fill a skyscraper. Blood flows through the body via a densely branching network consisting of 2,500 km of arteries, veins, and capillaries, equivalent to the distance from Paris to Moscow.

The heart must supply all organs with sufficient blood, while continually having to adjust its output to the actual load. When more blood is required, it responds by beating faster and by increasing the volume of blood pumped per contraction. The quantity of blood pumped by the heart during one beat, is defined as the **stroke volume** (approximately 70 cm^3 in the case of an adult at rest). At 70 beats per minute the daily volume pumped is 7,000 litres, enough to fill 40 bathtubs.

The heart is a maintenance-free pump which functions unattended throughout life, generally requiring no replacement parts. It drives the blood circulation, and has an exceptional ability to adjust its level of activity to differing loads. The volume of blood pumped per minute by one chamber can increase from 5 litres up to nearly 30 litres during strenuous muscular activity. This quantity is known as the **cardiac output**, usually expressed in litres per minute. It should be noted that both sides of the heart pump equal volumes of blood, otherwise large pressures would build up on one side of the circulatory system while the other side would receive too little blood.

The power output of the heart is approximately 1 Nm/s[1]. In the case of a machine the mass/power ratio is used to measure its efficiency. This means the mass required to produce for example 1 kW of energy. Taking the mass of the heart to be 0.3 kg, its mass/power ratio is (300 g)/(1 W) = 300 g/W = 300 kg/kW. Much lower values obtain for machines. For example:

Electric motor (at 1500 rev per min; 1 kW)	15 kg/kW
Marine diesel engine (large ship)	60 kg/kW
Diesel engine (heavy truck)	6 kg/kW
Four-stroke petrol engine (heavy vehicle)	1.6 kg/kW
Aeroplane engine (light construction)	0.6 kg/kW

But when working hard, the energy output of the heart can increase appreciably, so that its mass/power ratio approaches that of a mechanical pump.

The heart, a hollow muscular organ, is located in the cavity formed by connective tissue between the vertebral column and the breastbone. It is completely enclosed in a pouch called the pericardium, which extends between the pleural (lung lining) cavities on each side, from the diaphragm up to the large blood vessels. Normally the heart is one and a half times the size of one's fist, but it can be significantly larger in the case of trained athletes. Its mass is between 300 and 350 g, which is about 0.5 per cent of the body weight. In shape it resembles a rounded-off cone, the base of which is also the cardiac base. The septum separates the two halves of the heart, the right half serving the pulmonary circulation, whereas the left half independently pumps blood throughout the whole body. Oxygen-depleted blood from the entire body is received by the right half of the heart and passed on to the lungs (routes 2, 6, 7, 8 in the *diagram on page 51*). It is oxygenated in the lungs and subsequently flows to the left side of the heart where it is pumped in various directions through the body (routes 1, 3, 4, 5 in the *diagram on page 51*). The difference between arteries and veins is not determined by the quality of the blood, but by its flow direction to or away from the heart. Veins carry blood to the heart, while it is pumped away

---

[1] **Power:** In the SI system the Newton-metre per second is the unit used for expressing the amount of work divided by time. One Nm/s is equivalent to one Watt (in the case of electricity) and also to one Joule per second (the unit of heat transfer). We thus have: 1 Nm/s = 1 W = 1 J/s.

1. Arch of the aorta
2. Left pulmonary artery
3. Pulmonary veins (veins from the lungs)
4. Left atrium
5. Left coronary artery
6. Anterior branch of the left coronary artery
7. Large cardiac vein
8. Descending aorta
9. Anterior cardiac veins
10. Inferior vena cava
11. Right ventricle
12. Right coronary artery
13. Right atrium
14. Superior vena cava
15. Trachea

Anterior view of the heart and associated blood vessels

from the heart via the arteries. The arteries leading to the body carry oxygenated blood, while the blood in the veins lacks oxygen. This situation is reversed for the arteries leading to the lungs and the veins coming from the lungs.

Although the heart is filled with blood, it still requires its own blood supply. Situated on the surface of the heart, the branches of the coronary arteries penetrate its wall. The coronary veins collect blood from the capillaries in the heart muscles and carry it back. This circulatory route is the shortest in the entire human body.

Looking at the heart from the front, one actually sees mainly the right ventricle, with the right atrium above it. Two large veins (the *superior* and *inferior vena cava*; Latin *vena* = vein, *cava* = hollow) empty into the right atrium. The aorta arises from the left ventricle and arches over the pulmonary artery issuing from the right ventricle. It then passes downwards behind the heart.

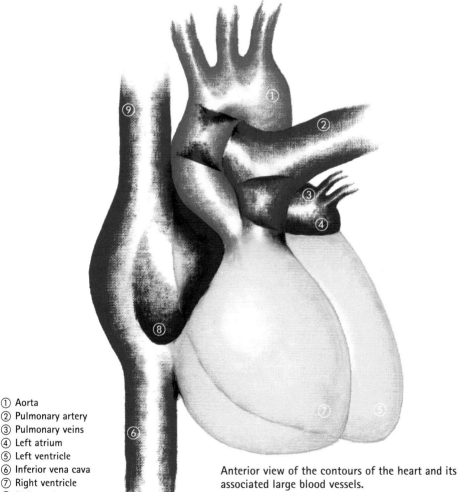

① Aorta
② Pulmonary artery
③ Pulmonary veins
④ Left atrium
⑤ Left ventricle
⑥ Inferior vena cava
⑦ Right ventricle
⑧ Right atrium
⑨ Superior vena cava

Anterior view of the contours of the heart and its associated large blood vessels.
The two halves can be readily distinguished: the right half is in the foreground, partially concealing the left half.

The pumping action of the heart is caused by a rhythmic alternation between relaxation and contraction. These are respectively known as the diastolic (Greek: *diastole* = expansion) and systolic (Greek: *systole* = contraction) actions of the ventricles (Latin: *ventriculus* = small chamber). During diastole the ventricles are filled with blood, and when they contract, the blood is forced into the main arteries. The four heart valves, situated at approximately the same level in rings of connective tissue, prevent the blood from flowing back.

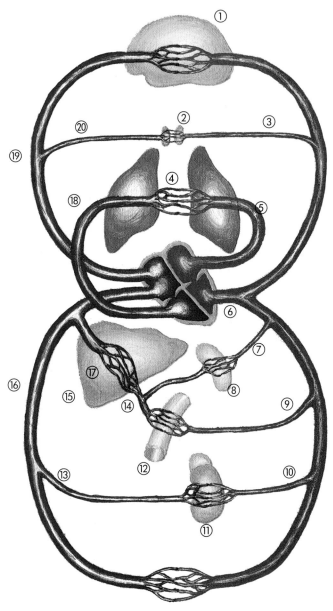

① Brain
② Thyroid gland
③ Thyroid artery
④ Pulmonary circulation
⑤ Pulmonary vein
⑥ Aorta
⑦ Splenic artery
⑧ Spleen
⑨ Superior mesenteric artery
⑩ Renal artery
⑪ Kidney
⑫ Intestine
⑬ Renal vein
⑭ Portal vein
⑮ Liver
⑯ Inferior vena cava
⑰ Hepatic veins
⑱ Pulmonary artery
⑲ Superior vena cava
⑳ Thyroid vein

The heart and the circulation of blood.
Schematic representation of the connections between the two halves of the heart and the minor (pulmonary) as well as the major (rest of the body) circulatory systems.

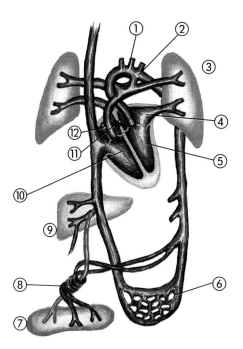

Foetal circulatory system.

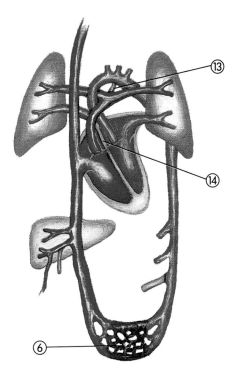

Neonatal circulatory system.

① Arch of the aorta
② Ductus arteriosus
③ Lung
④ Left atrium
⑤ Left ventricle
⑥ Bodily capillaries
⑦ Placenta
⑧ Umbilical blood vessels
⑨ Liver
⑩ Right ventricle
⑪ Foramen ovale
⑫ Right atrium
⑬ Closed ductus arteriosus
⑭ Closed foramen ovale

There are essential differences between the blood circulation of a foetus (above left), and that of a newborn (neonatal) baby (above right). Before birth the lungs of the foetus are unventilated, so the blood has to bypass the lungs. A major portion of the blood passes directly from the right atrium to the left through the foramen ovale, a hole in the atrial wall, thus bypassing the pulmonary circuit. That portion of the blood which flows through the right ventricle is passed from the pulmonary artery to the aorta via the ductus arteriosus, another bypass, and thus also avoids the pulmonary circuit. Before birth, the vital interchange of gases takes place in the placenta. The two umbilical arteries carry oxygen-depleted blood to the placenta, and oxygenated blood flows back to the foetus via the umbilical vein. After birth the lungs expand, giving rise to the pulmonary circuit because of the strongly increased flow of blood. At the same time the foramen ovale and the ductus arteriosus are closed, thus establishing the proper cycle of blood circulation.

The heart beats 70 times per minute, and pumps about 70 cm^3 of blood into the major circuit at each contraction. This means that the volume of blood pumped each minute is about 5 litres (70 x 70 = 4,900 cm^3). This is equal to the total volume of blood in the body. When physically active the muscles require more blood, so that the pressure and the flow volume of the blood increases. The volume per minute can then be raised to 25 litres, meaning that the entire blood volume is pumped through the body five times per minute. This is achieved by a doubling of the stroke volume from 70 to 140 cm^3 and the rate increases to as many as 180 beats per minute (140 x 180 = 25,200 cm^3 = 25 litres).

The human heart is morphologically and functionally a masterpiece of its Creator. The focal point of circulation, it responds to every demand, even from the most distant corners of the body. The larger blood vessels, arteries and veins, are the main roads carrying the necessary volumes of blood, but the capillaries provide the actual nourishment. In this cleverly designed network, the arteries branch repeatedly and supply the entire capillary network with blood. These capillaries in turn combine to form larger and larger veins.

The following table shows that 1,200 million capillaries, with a total length of 1,200 kilometres, must be supplied with blood.

Blood pressure: The pressure against which the left ventricle must push the blood, is called the *arterial blood pressure*. The resulting pressure waves can be felt as pulses when one touches the skin over a superficial artery. Arterial pressure changes continually, varying between a maximum systolic pressure (full contraction of the left ventricle) and a diastolic minimum (when the aortic valve is open). The *systolic pressure* is normally about 120 mm (in the old mercury pressure, which equals 16 kPa [2]), and the diastolic about 80 mm (= 10.7 kPa).

The **heart of a human embryo** already starts beating at 25 days after conception. Its size is then only 2.5 mm, while the embryo as such measures 6 mm. The heart of an adult man weighs about 320 g and that of a woman 270 g. It is noteworthy that the strict separation of the left (arterial) and the right (veinous) sides of the heart only commences at birth. In the foetus both atria are connected by the *foramen ovale* [3]. The Latin word *foetus* means begotten; in medical terms it refers to the embryo at four months and later.

Did you know that a near-instantaneous "change of heart" takes place directly after birth? The two halves of the heart of a foetus operate in parallel. Both atria and ventricles function together as a single hollow muscle, and the blood is oxygenated in the placenta. The lungs require very little blood, since they do not function, and they are

Type of vessel	Number	Total length (m)	Cross-sectional area (cm^2)	Diameter (mm)
Aorta	1	0.4	0.8	10.0
Large arteries	40	8	3	3.0
Arterial branches	600	60	5	1.0
Small art branches	1,800	18	5	0.6
Arterioles	40,000,000	80,000	125	0.02
Capillaries	1,200,000,000	1,200,000	600	0.008
Venules	80,000,000	160,000	570	0.03
Small vein branches	1,800	18	30	1.5
Venous tributaries	600	60	27	2.4
Large veins	40	8	11	6.0
Vena cava (superior and inferior)	2	0.4	1.2	12.5

Table 1: Numerical aspects of human blood vessels.

[2] **Pressure:** The SI unit for pressure is the Pascal (Pa), named after the French mathematician and physicist Blaise Pascal (1623 – 1662). 1 Pa = 1 N/m^2 = 1 kg/(ms^2). The previously used unit for air pressure, *millimetres of mercury* (mm Hg), was defined as follows in 1954 by the World Organisation for Metrology: "One mm Hg is the pressure exerted by a 1 mm column of mercury at a temperature of 0 °C and at a place where the gravitational acceleration is normal (9.80665 m/s^2)." The conversion factors are: 1 mm Hg = 133.332 Pa, 1 kPa = 1,000 Pa. In medicine, the old unit is used, for historical and practical reasons.

[3] **Foramen ovale** (Latin *foramen* = hole): The orifice in the septum between the two atria of a foetus.

"shunted on a siding" as far as blood circulation is concerned. After birth the two halves work in series. This changeover is effected by opening the pulmonary circuit and closing the foramen ovale between the left and the right vestibules, as well as closing the *ductus Botali* [4] between the aorta and the pulmonary artery. The Creator had planned this changeover from the parallel foetal operation of the two halves of the heart to serial functioning.

The Bible and the heart: Life depends on the regular beating of the heart, since it is the central organ of the circulatory system. It can be regarded as the bearer of life and it symbolically represents all vital organs. In biblical idiom the heart is the symbol of a person's essential being. Depression (Ps 34:18), sadness (John 16:6), worry (John 14:1), distress and anguish (2 Cor 2:4), but also joy (John 16:22), are attributed to the heart as the psycho-spiritual centre of life. "In his heart a man plans his course" (Prov 16:9), will and purpose spring from the heart (Nehemiah 4:6: "... the people worked with all their heart"), and other people can have a place in our hearts (2 Cor 7:3). Wisdom and truth, but also foolishness can live in the heart (1 Kings 3:12, Ps 14:1, Prov 22:15), just as love (1 Sam 18:1) and hate (Lev 19:17). Since the heart is the symbolic location of our feelings, the decision to be obedient or not (Acts 7:39) is also ascribed to it.

The functioning of the heart is investigated by a physician when he obtains an electro-cardiogram (ECG); in the same way God takes a spiritual ECG. He tests the faithfulness of our hearts: "The crucible for silver and the furnace for gold, but the LORD tests the heart" (Prov 17:3). Only God knows us inside and out, as David prays: "Search me, O God, and know my heart; test me and know my ... thoughts" (Ps 139:23).

Quotes:

French proverb: "There is no secret in our hearts which our behaviour does not reveal."

Chinese proverb: "Deep chasms can be filled, but never the human heart."

Hebrew proverb: "He who has a narrow heart, has a wide tongue. Any pain is better than that of the heart."

---

[4] **Ductus Botali** (Latin *ducere, ductum* = pull, lead; *ductus* = connecting passage; Leonardo Botalli was an Italian physician, 1530 – 1571): Ductus Botali = ductus arteriosus = connection between the pulmonary artery and the aorta of a foetus.

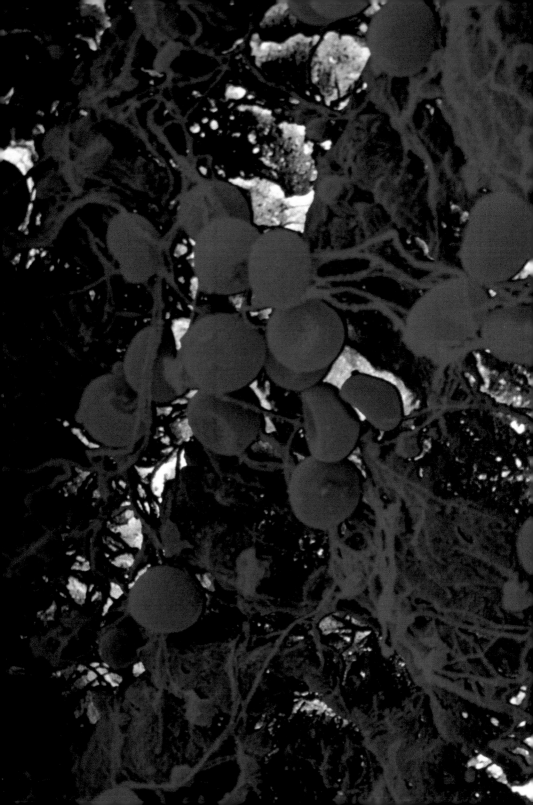

The blood

– a universal transport medium

The blood (Latin *sanguis*, Greek *haima*) is the great transport medium of the body. While circulating, this liquid [1] performs several important functions:

1 *Respiration:* The blood carries oxygen from the lungs to all body tissues for them to utilise. At the same time carbon dioxide is carried from the tissues back to the lungs where it is exhaled. This vital function is mainly performed by the red blood cells.

2 *Nourishment:* The cells of the body continually require energy and raw materials, and the blood plays an all-important part by transporting nutrients to the individual cells of the body. The products resulting from the digestion of food are absorbed by the blood from the gut (mainly the small intestine). The length of the small intestine is between five and seven metres, and its total surface area exceeds that of the lungs. If one were to iron out all its protuberances, its area would be larger than a tennis court. Nutrients, dissolved in water, are collected by the blood from the small intestine and carried to the liver along the portal vein (*vena portae*). Consisting of a patchwork of about 100,000 hexagonal pieces called lobules (hepatic lobule, Greek *hepar* =

liver), the liver is the largest internal organ. The basic metabolism of the body takes place in the liver. Employing unique and wonderful processes, the cells of the lobules chemically convert sugar, fats, proteins, and other nutrients. The products are either stored, re-used, or released. About 30 per cent of the blood leaving the heart passes through the liver, and from there the nutrients are distributed throughout the body.

The blood plays another important role in nutrition: Superfluous nutrients are stored in certain "depots" and transported to active cells when required.

3 *Excretory function:* The end products of cellular metabolism diffuse into the interstitial spaces between the cells and from there to the blood. These chemicals are then filtered out by the excretory organs, mainly the kidneys. (*Excretion* = the removal or elimination of metabolic products (excreta) which cannot be used by the body, like urine and sweat; in contrast, the process of *secretion* produces substances which the body needs.)

4 *The control of concentrations:* The cells of the body can only function optimally when the prevailing internal conditions are within certain limits (eg. the concentration of dissolved substances should be constant, as well as the temperature and the acid-base ratio). Certain organs continually monitor these blood values and correct them when necessary. The composition of the intercellular liquids is kept in equilibrium by interchanges with the blood.

5 *Temperature control:* At the normal temperature of the body, 37 °C, all processes function optimally. The organs generate heat, but the main component of the blood, water, has a high specific heat value, so that the heat capacity of blood is also high. Furthermore, since the blood flows continually, the transfer of heat is much faster than in the case of a non-moving liquid. On the one hand, the blood absorbs any excess heat, which is then dissipated over the surface of the body and through the lungs. On the other hand, circulation of the blood ensures that all parts of the body receive the necessary heat.

---

[1] **Measures of volume:** Many types of volume are mentioned in this chapter, and the following conversion table may be useful in this respect:

1 cubic metre = 1 m^3 = 1000 dm^3 = 1000 l
1 cubic decimetre = 1 dm^3 = 1 litre
1 cubic centimetre = 1 cm^3 = 1000 mm^3 = 1 millilitre
1 cubic millimetre = 1 mm^3 = 10^9 μm^3
1 cubic micrometre = 1 μm^3 = 1 thousand millionth of a mm^3
1 litre = 1 l = 1 dm^3 = 1000 cm^3 = 1000 ml = 100 cl
1 centilitre = 1 cl = 10 ml
1 millilitre = 1 ml = 1 cm^3 = 1000 μl
1 microlitre = 1 μl = 1 mm^3

6 *Transportation of hormones:* The blood also conveys the body's own chemicals, which are collected from their points of origin or their places of storage. Various hormones (Greek *horman* = drive, excite) are secreted by the endocrine glands (Greek *éndon* = inside, *krinein* = separate, excrete). Many vital processes are controlled by special substances in the blood, known as hormones. They are produced in certain tissues or glands, taken up by the blood, and transported to other specific tissues or organs, often located at considerable distances. There they perform functions vital to the organism, although they appear only in minute quantities in the blood.

Some hormones are:
Adrenalin – secreted when the sympathetic nerves are excited, causing blood vessels to contract.
Renin and *angiotensin* – control of blood pressure.
Histamine – plays an important role in antigen/antibody reactions.
Somatotropin – growth hormone
Insulin – controls the processing of the glucose absorbed in the intestine, as well as that synthesised by the body itself.
Male and female sexual hormones.
Cortisone – controls (among other things) the immune response.
Thyroid hormones – control heat and metabolism.

7 *Defence:* The leucocytes (white blood cells) and certain chemicals (antibodies) protect the body against toxins and intruding micro-organisms.

8 *Coagulation:* Blood coagulation affords a vitally important protection against loss of blood; it also repairs damaged blood vessels.

Obviously, the blood carries out vitally important functions. It is the *raison d'être* as well as the handmaiden of the circulatory system. It supplies each and every cell with fuel (obtained from the nutrients we ingest), with oxygen, with vitamins, with hormones, and with warmth. Metabolic products and excess heat are also carried away from every cell. Blood flows ceaselessly throughout our lifetime. It does not collect at specific points, but flows in a never-ending loop through the circulatory system. Filling and emptying itself every second with blood, the heart is the centre of this system.

Composition of the blood: Blood plasma (the liquid component) comprises 56 % of the blood, and solid particles (the blood corpuscles) make up the other 44 %. Three types of corpuscles can be distinguished:

Red blood corpuscles

- Red blood cells (= *erythrocytes*; Greek *erythrós* = red; *kytos* = hollowed, convex).
  Quantity: 4.5 – 5 million per mm³ blood
- White blood corpuscles (*leucocytes*; Greek *leukós* = bright, shiny, white).
  Quantity: 4,000 – 10,000 per mm³ blood
  Three types can be distinguished: lymphocytes (30 %), granulocytes (66 %), and monocytes (4 %)
- Platelets (*thrombocytes*; Greek *thrómbos* = coagulated blood)
  Quantity: 150,000 – 350,000 per mm³ blood

Red blood corpuscles: Did you know that every drop of blood contains 250 million red cells? During its average lifespan of 120 days each of these highly specialised cells performs an extremely important task: it absorbs oxygen 175,000 times, and discharges carbon dioxide the same number of times. Its diameter is close to one thousandth of a millimetre. If all 25 million

million erythrocytes contained in the 5 litres of a man's blood were laid side by side, their total area would cover 3,800 square metres, more than half of a football field.

Human erythrocytes are circular disks, concave on both sides. Their greatest thickness at the edge is about 2 µm and the average diameter is

24 hours. The production rate is thus 160 million per minute, or 230,000 million per day. This amounts to 2.7 million per second – an astounding rate!

One of the most important tasks of the blood is to transport the oxygen absorbed in the lungs to all organs and tissues, at the same time convey-

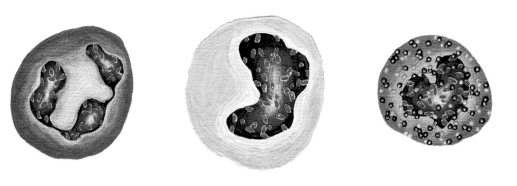

Neutrophilic granulocyte   Monocyte   Basophilic granulocyte

7.5 µm (normocyte). The central cross-sectional shape is like a dumb-bell, only 1 µm thick at the centre. This characteristic shape provides for the greatest diffusion area. It also optimally serves another purpose: They are easily distorted and are thus able to pass through narrow, curved capillaries. They can even pass through blood vessels with a smaller diameter than the average erythrocyte. Having a volume of 90 µm³, their biconcave disk shape has an area of 140 µm², but if they were spherical, the area would have been only 97 µm².

Erythrocytes do not have a cellular nucleus, so they are unable to divide and replicate. This means that all red blood cells have to be replaced at the end of their lifetime. This renewal, known as *erythropoesis* (Greek *poesis* = regeneration) takes place in the bone marrow. It should be noted that about 0.9 % of the total complement of 25 million million red blood corpuscles are renewed every

The various blood cells. *The blood cells are produced in the red bone marrow from a common stem cell, the haemocytoblast, and are released into the surrounding blood after a certain maturation period. Except for the lymphocytes, which also reproduce in the lymphatic organs, all blood cells are produced in the red bone marrow throughout our lifetime.*

ing the carbon dioxide (CO_2) produced there back to the lungs. The erythrocytes are essentially responsible for this function of the blood. The red pigment **hemoglobin** (abbr. Hb) has the ability to absorb oxygen in the lung capillaries and subsequently release it in the capillaries of the body tissues. It is also able to bind some of the carbon dioxide produced by cellular metabolism and release it in the lungs. Hemoglobin thus plays a central role in the transportation of respiratory gases. It is a protein comprising 34 per cent of the wet weight of the erythrocytes, water being the most abundant component.

One cell contains 32 pg (1 picogram = 10^{-12} g) hemoglobin, comprising about 300 million molecules. This red pigment comprises about 95 % of the dry weight of erythrocytes. Interestingly, the 32 pg per cell in an adult organism is practically a universal constant for the animal kingdom. In terms of volume the quantity of Hb is about 140 g/l for adult women, and 160 g/l for men.

Consisting of four pyrrole rings connected by methine bridges (– CH =), the heme has a bivalent iron atom at its centre. Oxygen can be attached to the central iron atom without changing its chemical valence. The Creator designed this amazing structure without which human life would not have been possible. Consider the following:

Eosinophilic granulocyte

Platelets (thrombocytes)

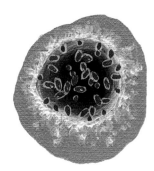

Small lymphocyte

The body thus has a total quantity of between 700 and 960 grams of Hb available in its 5 to 6 litres of blood. The percentage of iron in hemoglobin is 0.334 %, so that 3 grams, or 70 %, of all the iron in the body is located in the hemoglobin.

Each of these Hb molecules is a complex protein, consisting of *globin* (Greek *globus* = sphere) which is connected to an iron-containing pigment component, *heme* (Greek *haima* = blood) by means of four polypeptide chains. Because of the four chains this protein is known as a tetrameric protein (Greek *tetra* = four). Two of these chains consist of 141 amino acids (the α chain), and the other two have 146 amino acids (the β chain). The normal hemoglobin for an adult is indicated by Hb-$\alpha_2\beta_2$ or simply HbA. The exact sequence of the amino acids in the chains is of crucial importance for the structure of the globin molecule. Small deviations can seriously affect its function.

Normally, in the presence of water and oxygen, the iron in *free heme* is immediately oxidised to tri-valent iron (hematin); it cannot then absorb any oxygen. The Creator prevented this futile reaction by shaping the globin chain to form a protective coat. This chain also has other important functional properties:

In the *first* place the absorption of oxygen is reversible, since it does not depend on a chemical bond. If a chemical bond had to be severed, energy would have been required. *Secondly*, the quantity of oxygen to be absorbed or released can be regulated, making it possible to supply varying levels of oxygen to peripheral organs according to their physiological requirements. It can also be stated thus: Human life could not have existed without the finely tuned properties of hemoglobin, which are the result of its well designed molecular structure.

The entire molecule, consisting of 10,000 atoms, has a molecular weight of about 68,000 (compare: H_2O: 18, CO_2: 44, insulin: 41,000). It is precisely folded in such a way as to obtain its characteristic near-spherical shape (diameter: 5.5 nm, 1 nm = 10^{-9} m). Each of its four equal sized parts is also roughly spherical.

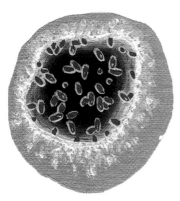

Large lymphocyte

When oxygenated, the colour of the blood changes from dull purplish (the venous blood depleted of oxygen) to a bright scarlet (the colour of oxygen-rich arterial blood). Oxygenated Hb is known as *oxy-hemoglobin*. The theoretical oxygen capacity of the 5 – 6 litres of blood in the body is between 1,100 and 1,400 ml, but only 25 % of this amount is actually utilised. In an equal volume of water (5 – 6 litres) at 20 °C only 150 – 180 ml oxygen can be dissolved (and even less at 37 °C). When carbon monoxide (CO) is inhaled, it replaces oxygen, because it binds more tightly with Hb. This explains the high toxity of even small concentrations of CO in the air.

A fraction of the oxygen is transported by the blood in the form of dissolved O_2, as is the case with other respiratory gases. Although this quantity of oxygen (0.3 ml per 100 ml blood) is minute, it is quite important, since oxygen can only diffuse into body tissues when it is physically dissolved. But most of the oxygen transported by the blood is bound to Hb, maximally in the ratio of four oxygen molecules per molecule of Hb. It follows that one gram of Hb can absorb 1.36 ml oxygen (Hüfner's number). The average man has 15.3 g of Hb per 100 ml blood, and a woman has 14.5 g Hb, so that each 100 ml of a man's blood can carry 20.8 ml O_2 (19.7 ml in the case of a woman), when all the heme is fully oxygenated. Hb thus transports 70 times as much oxygen as that which can be physically dissolved in the serum. The total amount of Hb in 5.5 litres of blood is between about 745 and 820 g.

Some noteworthy numbers:

The total number of red blood corpuscles:	25 million million
That is,	
– in one cubic millimetre (mm^3):	5,000,000
– in one drop of blood:	250,000,000
– in one cubic cm (cm^3):	5,000,000,000
Total surface area of all red blood cells:	3,800 m^2
Total number of white blood cells:	35,000 million
Total number of platelets:	1.25 million million

To get some visual grasp of the immense number of erythrocytes in our body: If all these red blood cells were stacked one on top of the other, the stack would reach a height of 40,000 km, the circumference of the earth at the equator. If all 25 million million red blood corpuscles were laid down next to one another, we would have a 190,000 km long band which would be nearly five times the circumference of the earth.

The red blood cells differ before and after birth: It is amazing that different kinds of hemoglobin are synthesised in the embryonic stage (up to the third month), the fetal stage until birth, and the adult stage. Special circulatory and metabolic requirements have to be met by the hemoglobin at each stage. This is achieved by changing the tetramers (the four protein chains) in the Hb molecule. There are two more types in addition to the *alpha* and *beta* chains mentioned above, namely *epsilon* and *gamma* chains. During the third month of pregnancy the **embryonic**

hemoglobin having two alpha and two epsilon tetramers (called $Hb\alpha_2\varepsilon_2$), is replaced by **fetal** hemoglobin which has two alpha and two gamma chains (designated by $Hb\alpha_2\gamma_2$). During its development the fetus requires abundant quantities of oxygen. Note that respiratory gases and energy-rich substances are interchanged in the placenta [2]. The partial pressure [3] of the oxygen in the blood coming from the placenta is only 4,270 Pa, more or less equal to that prevailing in arteries at a height of 10,000 m. This is far below the normal value of 21,278 Pa. If the fetus had the normal adult-type hemoglobin (HbA, A = adult), its blood would have been only 60 % saturated because of the low partial pressure of the oxygen. The Creator thus provided a structurally different hemoglobin at this stage, called fetal hemoglobin (HbF, F = fetal). It has special oxygen carrying properties attuned to the coupling between the fetal circulation and that of the mother. Because of its special structure, Hbf is able to absorb 20-30 % more oxygen than HbA.

The process of converting fetal hemoglobin, HbF, into HbA (containing two alpha and two beta chains), begins some time before birth, so that at birth only between 60 and 80 per cent fetal hemoglobin remains. The process is completed about three months after birth. It is astounding how all these processes occur purposefully when and where necessary to meet changing requirements.

Leucocytes: The leucocytes, also known as white blood cells or white blood corpuscles, are much less abundant than the erythrocytes. There are only between 4,000 and 10,000 of them in one mm^3, and their number is variable. They increase after a meal or after physical activity. There are morphologically different kinds of leucocytes; their purpose is to defend the body against intruders, each in its own particular way, and to defend it to the death, as it were. They die by the millions wherever there is a point of entry for infection. There are about six thousand million white corpuscles in every litre of blood, one for every 600 to 1,000 red blood cells. In contrast to the latter, the leucocytes are complete cells having a nucleus as well as organelles. They are also known as *granulocytes*, because in large concentrations the blood plasma appears to be granular. Five types can be distinguished, three according to their ability to be stained. Sixty per cent of the leucocytes are *neutrophilic* granulocytes (Greek *philos* = friend; they are readily stained by neutral dyes), five per cent are *eosinophilic* (Greek *eos* = the rosiness of dawn; eosin is a red dye used for microscopic analysis), and two per cent are *basophilic* (they can be stained with basic dyes). The remaining two kinds of white blood cells are the *lymphocytes* (30 %) and the *monocytes* (3 %).

The leucocyte army is an impressive team of specialists. While half of them are patrolling within the blood, the others are on external duty, guarding the tissues. Bacteria, viruses, fungi and parasites continually enter our bodies through breaches of the skin, in the air we breathe, and

---

[2] **Placenta** (Latin: flat cake): Because of continued growth, the embryo cannot acquire sufficient nourishment and oxygen by means of diffusion, nor can it succesfully eliminate CO_2 and other metabolic substances. For these reasons a placenta develops during pregnancy. It is a spongy growth which handles the interchange of substances between mother and fetus. On the one hand fetal blood must come very close to that of the mother to enable the required interchanges, but, on the other hand, the two kinds of blood cannot be allowed to mix, otherwise the mother's immune reactions would attack the fetus. This problem is solved in the placenta by the diffusion of gases and foodstuffs between intertwined capillaries. The umbilical cord connects the placenta to the fetus, and the placenta is ejected after birth.

[3] **Partial pressure**: The partial pressure of a gas is the pressure it exerts in a mixture of gases. The mixture exerts a certain total pressure, and each different gas contributes its share accordingly. Expressed quantitatively, it means that the measured total pressure of a mixture of gases is equal to the sum of all the pressures exerted by each gas in the mixture. The normal pressure at sea level is 101,325 Pascal (Pa), and when dry, air contains 21 % oxygen. This means that the partial pressure of the oxygen, indicated by PO_2, is $0.21 \times 101,325$ Pa $= 21,278$ Pa.

from food in the alimentary canal. They are recognised as enemies, and, when located, the army goes into action. The basophilic granulocytes and the lymphocytes fire chemical weapons at them. Next on the scene are the neutrophils, the eosinophils, and the monocytes. They individually surround the intruders and absorb and digest them. Remarkably, this secret army is able to clearly distinguish between friend and foe, between the body's own substances and foreign matter.

Thrombocytes: A healthy adult has between 150,000 and 350,000 platelets in a cubic mm of blood. These thrombocytes have no nucleus, they are flat, and are irregularly rounded in shape. They measure between 1 and 4 μm in length, with a thickness of 0.5 – 0.75 μm, and comprise cell fragments enclosed in a membrane. Continuously replenished by the bone marrow, their average lifespan is between 5 and 11 days. They are normally inactive, but can be activated by contact with e.g. roughened surfaces, such as when a blood vessel is cut or injured, and by certain blood coagulation factors. When activated, they are able to release substances necessary for blood clotting. When blood loss commences through injury, many platelets accumulating together form a mass which "plugs" the defect. In the process, they disintegrate, releasing substances that trigger off coagulation.

The Bible and blood: Having explored the fundamental importance of the blood for all physiological processes in the body, we now have an entirely new approach to biblical passages which mention blood. We read in Deuteronomy 12:23: "the blood is the life". Consistent with what we have now learned of the vital role of blood, the Bible regards blood as the seat of life.

After Cain had killed his brother Abel, God accused him with the words: "Your brother's *blood cries out* to me from the ground" (Gen 4:10). In Genesis 37:27 the following turn of phrase is used to indicate family relationship: "... our own flesh and blood". Human life is precious to God, Who prohibits human sacrifice (Deut 18:10) and cannibalism. Anybody who sheds

human blood, violates God's image and thus the Creator Himself, Who will then avenge the shed blood: "Whoever sheds the blood of man, by man shall his blood be shed; for in the image of God has God made man" (Gen 9:6). God empowered human authorities to fulfil this task; they have been commissioned by God to bear the sword to redress evil. When the authorities justly punish evildoers, they do so for our benefit (Rom 13:1-4).

The blood of the martyrs (the prophets and others who were witnesses for Jesus) is especially mentioned. In Matthew 23:35 Jesus accuses the scribes and the pharisees: "And so upon you will come all the righteous blood that has been shed on earth, from the blood of righteous Abel..." In Revelation the blood of the witnesses of Jesus is mentioned often, those who lost their lives for the sake of the Word of God (Rev 6:10, 16:6, 17:6, 18:24, and 19:2).

In the Old Testament God emphasises the value of blood. Before the exodus of the Israelites from Egypt, God told them to smear the blood of the passover lamb on the tops and sides of their doorframes. "The blood will be a sign for you on the houses where you are; and when I see the blood, I will pass over you. No destructive plague will touch you when I strike Egypt" (Exodus 12:13). In all other houses the firstborn died.

This was a concealed reference to the saving blood of the perfect Lamb, namely the **blood of Jesus**. In the eyes of God there is no forgiveness without the shedding of blood (Hebrews 9:22). The Son of God thus had to be incarnated in human form to bring the **only** sacrifice that could save us. After He had risen from the dead, He asked the disciples going to Emmaus: "Did not the Christ **have to suffer** these things and then enter his glory?" (Luke 24:26). The *blood of Jesus* (Hebr 10:19, 1 John 1:7) as well as all its synonyms like the *blood of Jesus Christ* (1 Peter 1:2), the *blood of Christ* (1 Cor 10:16, Eph 2:13, and Hebr 9:14), and the *blood of the Lord* (1 Cor 11:27), occupy a central place in the New Testament. All these concepts are abbreviations for the blood shed by Jesus Christ, his death and self-sacrifice on the cross of Calvary for the sins of a lost humanity. The real meaning of the blood of Jesus can be summarised as follows:

1 The blood which Jesus shed for us is the price He paid for our salvation. It is the only way of obtaining eternal life: "For you know that it was not with perishable things such as silver or gold that you were redeemed..., but with the precious blood of Christ" (1 Peter 1:18-19). "Nothing impure will ever enter it (heaven)..., but only those whose names are written in the Lamb's book of life" (Rev 21:27). We can only enter heaven when we are purified, and this has been accomplished by Jesus: "The blood of Jesus, his Son, purifies us from all sin" (1 John 1:7).

2 The sacrifice of Jesus paid our debts before God. Not only are our personal sins taken away, but Jesus bore the punishment for the entire lost human race: "Look, the Lamb of God, who takes away the sin of the world" (John 1:29). The wide-reaching impact of Jesus' act of redemption is expressed clearly in Romans 5:18: "Just as the result of one trespass was condemnation for all men, so also the result of one act of righteousness was justification that brings life for all men." His sacrifice is sufficient for all humanity. Unfortunately only a few avail themselves of this opportunity (see Matthew 7:13-14, and paragraph 7 below).

3 The result of man's sin was a deep, unbridgeable chasm between the holy God and sinful man. But through Jesus we are redeemed in the sight of God, "by making peace through his blood, shed on the cross" (Col 1:20b), and we may now have fellowship with the Father and with his Son, Jesus Christ (1 John 1:3).

4 The blood of Jesus sealed the "New Covenant": "In the same way, after the supper He took the cup, saying, This cup is the new covenant in my blood, which is poured out for you" (Luke 22:20). Our fellowship with Jesus Christ becomes visible in the Lord's supper. We must always remind ourselves of his sacrifice: "This is my body, which is for you; do this in remembrance of me... This cup is the new covenant in my blood; do this, whenever you drink it, in remembrance of me" (1 Cor

11:24-25). At the same time it proclaims a message lasting until His second coming: "For whenever you eat this bread and drink this cup, you proclaim the Lord's death until he comes" (1 Cor 11:26).

5 Jesus' sacrifice protects us from all future judgments of God: "Since we have now been justified by his blood, how much more shall we be saved from God's wrath through him!" (Rom 5:9).

6 With His blood Christ saved and freed us from the power of the devil and of all other evil forces. We have also been liberated from the slavery of sin; the enemy cannot touch us any more. The blood of Jesus conquered all hostile powers, and we may also live in this victory: "Death has been swallowed up in victory. Where, O death, is your victory? Where, O death, is your sting? ... But thanks be to God! He gives us the victory through our Lord Jesus Christ" (1 Cor 15:54, 55, 57). We are protected against the wiles, the temptations, and the violence of the enemy. It is said of those who have suffered severe adversions but kept their faith to the end: "They overcame him [the accuser, the enemy] by the blood of the Lamb and by the word of their testimony; they did not love their lives so much as to shrink from death" (Rev 12:11).

7 Although Jesus' act has redemptive power for all people, it still has to be accepted personally. His sacrifice is not all-inclusively, automatically valid for everybody. God only gives His forgiveness, His salvation, His peace, and Himself to those who really desire it. He regards our free will very seriously, so that his great gifts are only available to *those who* "call on the name of the Lord", *only they* "will be saved" (Acts 2:21).

64

Quote:

Dr Don Batten, B.Sc. Agr. (Hons), Ph.D.,
in the magazine *Creation ex nihilo*
(Vol. 19, No. 2, 1997, p. 25):

"Blood was originally created to do what it does
and what it does do it does marvellously well –
just as it was designed to do! Such a complex
system did not arise through a series of accidents
following the enclosure of some seawater, as
some evolutionists might want to believe. Nor
can accidents improve it – they only destroy. Let
us give our Creator, the Lord Jesus Christ, the
honour that is rightfully His for creating our
blood with all ist wonderful functions!"

65

66

The kidneys

– marvels of filtration

The human kidney, weighing between 120 and 160 g, is a complex physico-chemical factory which is essential for purifying the blood (Diagram p 68). The two kidneys are located on either side of the backbone in the region of the loins. They control the fluid balance of the body and keep constant the composition and volume of the extra-cellular liquid in which all the cells of the body are bathed. In this way the functioning of all the cells of the body is optimised. When there is too much liquid or too much of dissolved substances, the kidneys ensure that excesses are eliminated. If there is a shortage of water, the kidneys reduce the excretion of water without affecting the essential elimination of metabolic end-products. All these processes are carried out in such a way that the kidneys control the water and salt content of the blood and excrete the waste products of protein metabolism (urea) and purine metabolism (uric acid), as well as any toxins.

For this purpose, blood flows through the kidneys at an astounding rate – 1.2 litres of blood each minute, which is four times their own weight. The specific perfusion of an organ is a term indicating the amount of blood flowing through it per minute in proportion to its weight. This amounts to $(1,200 \text{ cm}^3 \text{ blood/min})/(280 \text{ g kidney weight}) = 4.3 \text{ cm}^3/(\text{g} \times \text{min})$. This is appreciably higher than for the other major organs like the brain, liver, or heart muscle. Every day 1,700 litres of blood flow through the kidneys. This is more than twenty times the entire body weight and 340 times the total amount of blood in the body, which is about 5 litres. The quantity of blood passing through the kidneys in one hour is 15 times the entire volume of the blood in the circulatory system.

There are about 2.5 million renal glomeruli (Latin singular *glomerulus* = the diminutive of *glomus* = cluster; plural: *glomeruli*) which, together with a similar quantity of renal tubules (having a total length of nearly 100 km), contribute to a cleverly designed physical filtering process, actually a molecular sieve.

The volume of liquid filtered by the glomeruli per unit of time provides a measure of the excretory capacity of the kidneys. This is called the glomerular filtration rate (GFR) which is about 120 cm^3 per minute. This means that approximately 180 litres, which is 60 times as much as the volume of all the blood plasma (the liquid part of the blood, being about three litres), are filtered and purified every day. The total volume of extra-cellular fluid in the body (including blood) is about 14 litres, so even this amount passes 13 times per day through the kidney filter. The renal glomeruli thus excrete 180 litres of ultra-filtrate (primary urine) per day. This high volume is required to properly excrete metabolic products through the capillary walls. But if this enormous quantity of urine were passed directly, the water loss would be horrendous. This volume of urine would fill 18 buckets a day, and we would never be able to leave the toilet. What's more, we would have to drink a similar quantity of water each day.

However, the all-wise Creator set up an ingenious principle whereby more than 99 per cent of the water and the major portion of other vital substances are returned to the body. As the filtrate travels further along the renal tubules (diagram page 69), water, glucose, and sodium chloride are recovered and returned to the blood. The recovery ratio is about 100:1, so that only between 1 and 1.6 litres of urine are eliminated, depending on the quantity of ingested liquid and on other water losses (e. g. sweat).

In cross-section (diagram p 69), the kidney displays an outer granular cortex and an inner, radially striped medullary layer. The nephron (Greek *nephron* = kidney) is the smallest functional renal unit. It comprises the glomerulus, together with the blood-transporting arterioles, the renal tubule, and the papillary duct (left part of the diagram on page 68). Granular in appearance, the renal glomeruli are an extremely well-designed apparatus. The vas afferens[1] (diameter between 20 and 50 μm), conveying the incoming blood, branches into a bundle of very fine capillaries with a diameter of only 7 μm = 0.007 mm. The tiny vessels in this clump (about 30 loops; see the right hand part of the diagram on page 69) subsequently combine to form the vas efferens which carries the blood away. This is a marvellously constructed system.

The tuft of blood vessels is enclosed in a double-walled container known as Bowman's capsule, whose diameter is only about 0.17 mm. The place where the blood enters and leaves, is called the vascular pole. The urinary pole, where a single conduit emerges, is located at the other end of

¹ **Vas afferens, vas efferens** (Latin *vas* = vessel; *affere* = bring in; *effere* = take away): The vas afferens leads from the interlobular arteries into the renal glomerulus, and the vas efferens leads back out of the glomerulus.

the capsule. The walls of the looped capillaries act like a filter with extremely fine pores. These allow water and other small molecules to be squeezed out through them, but blood corpuscles and large protein molecules cannot pass through.

The result of this ultra-filtration is that 180 litres of "primary" urine is pressed from 1,700 litres of blood during a 24 hour period, comprising a loss of about 10 per cent by volume. But most of this "loss" is recovered by means of the retro-absorption taking place in the renal tubules, tiny tubes which extend from the urinary poles of the capsules. Water, glucose, and other substances are recovered from the primary urine and returned to the blood. A renal tubule starts with a convoluted segment which joins directly to a straight seg-

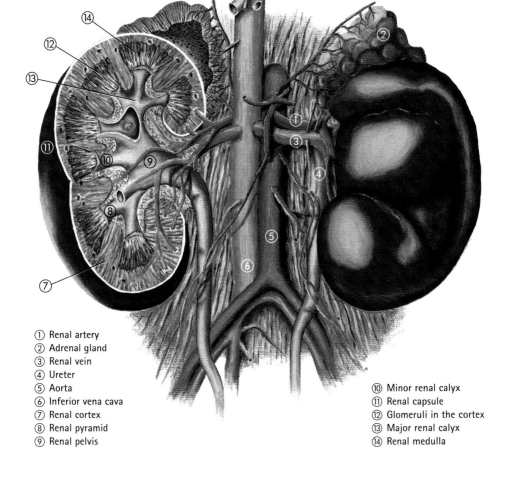

1. Renal artery
2. Adrenal gland
3. Renal vein
4. Ureter
5. Aorta
6. Inferior vena cava
7. Renal cortex
8. Renal pyramid
9. Renal pelvis
10. Minor renal calyx
11. Renal capsule
12. Glomeruli in the cortex
13. Major renal calyx
14. Renal medulla

ment, followed by the thin loop of Henle. This leads into another convoluted segment, the distal tubule (see the left diagram on page 69). This discharges urine into a minor collecting duct, which becomes a larger collecting tube (the papillary duct). Bundles of these end in bulges of the renal medulla *(renal papillae)*. These in turn are incorporated in cuplike extensions *(renal calyces)* of the renal pelvis (diagram page 68), where they discharge their urine. This is subsequently carried to the bladder by the ureter.

Continual contemplation of God's Word acts in our lives like purifying kidneys, as Jesus told his disciples: "You are already clean because of the word I have spoken to you" (John 15:3). The redemptive power of the blood of Jesus is the foundation of purification; in the Word of God the church is told that "Christ loved the church and gave himself up to her to make her holy, cleansing her by washing with water through the Word" (Eph 5:25-26).

We cannot live without kidneys. If someone's sins have not been forgiven, and all the accumulated dross is not eliminated, then he is spiritually dead. Nobody can have everlasting life without spiritual kidneys, as Jesus said: "Let the (spiritually) dead bury their own (physically) dead" (Matt 8:22).

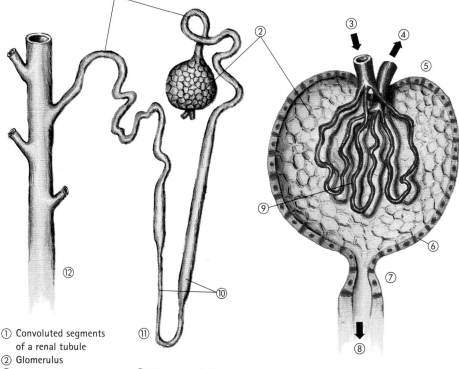

① Convoluted segments of a renal tubule
② Glomerulus
③ Incoming blood
④ Outgoing blood
⑤ Vascular pole
⑥ Bowman's capsule (diameter 0.17 mm)
⑦ Urinary pole
⑧ Primary urine
⑨ Glomerular tuft (capillaries)
⑩ Straight (ascending and descending) segments of the tubule
⑪ Loop of Henle
⑫ Papillary duct

Detail of a human kidney.
Left: A nephron, the functional unit
Right: Enlarged cross-sectional view
of a renal glomerulus

69

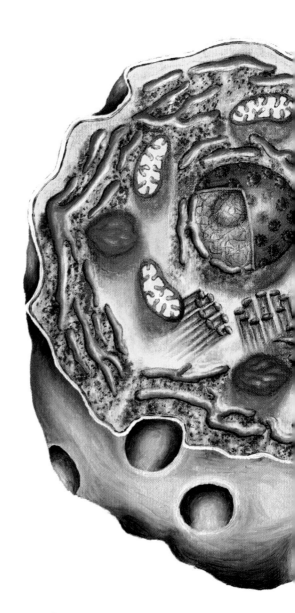

The cells

Simplified representation of a cell

1. Centriole
2. Cellular wall
3. Rough endoplasmic reticulum (containing ribosomes)
4. Lysosome
5. Nucleolus
6. Chromosomes
7. Nucleus
8. Mitochondrion
9. Golgi bodies
10. Cytoplasm

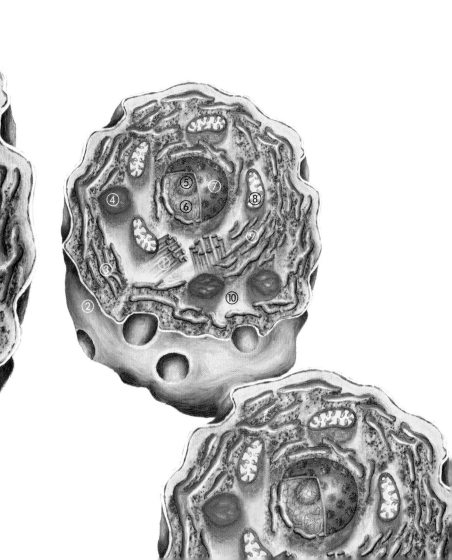

The cells

– our body's 100 million million building blocks

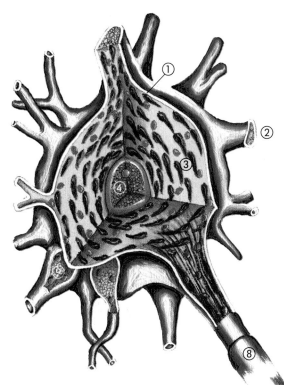

Did you know that the human body consists of approximately 100 million million cells, each of which contains 10,000 times as many molecules as there are stars in the Milky Way? Note that the Milky Way comprises at least 100,000 million stars.

The smallest building blocks of the human body, as well as of plants and animals, are the cells. Body structures consist of cells, along with inter-cellular material. In the case of unicellular organisms (protozoa), the cell is the entire organism. A cell is the smallest possible morphological entity capable of independent life. In metazoa (many-celled creatures) the cells are the basic functional organic units, or building blocks, which make up the whole organism. Cells differ widely in regard to size, shape, and function.

1. Cell membrane
2. Section of a dendrite
3. Cytoplasm with mitochondria and endoplasmic reticulum
4. Nucleus with nucleolus
5. Post-synaptic unit
6. Synaptic vesicles
7. Node of Ranvier
8. Myelin sheath
9. Pre-synaptic nerve terminal

Schematic diagram of a neural (nerve) cell.

72

Size: The sizes of human cells vary considerably. Very few of them are visible to the unaided eye or with a magnifying glass. The largest cells, the ova (egg cells), become just barely visible at a diameter of 0.15 mm (150 µm) or more. (1 µm = 1 micrometre = 1 thousandth of a millimetre). Many of the larger neural (nerve) cells have a diameter of between 0.12 and 0.2 mm = 120 to 200 µm. Many neural cells have extensions (processes) up to one metre or more in length, but their diameter is only a few micrometres. The sizes of most other human cells vary between 5 µm and 20 µm, depending on the tissue type. Even so, some neural cells and some giant cells in bone marrow can measure up to 80 µm or more, several times the average cell size. Measuring 4 to 5 µm, the glial cells (Latin *glia* = glue) are, along with sperm cells, among the smallest human cells. The diameter of the "heads" of sperm cells is between 3 and 5 µm. With their average diameter of 7.5 µm, the red blood corpuscles also count among the smallest cells. The median cell size is between 30 and 50 µm.

Shape: Because of their special functions the shapes of most cells differ widely. They are eminently suited to their locality. Cells occurring in covering layers, like an epithelium, can be cubical, flat, or prismatic, and are as densely packed as their shapes allow. Many cells are spherical, or spindle shaped like those in the smooth muscle tissue. Nerve and connective tissue cells can have long, branching processes.

Multitasking: Even though the basic plan of all cells is the same, they may differ significantly according to their function. Every kind of cell is specialised to perform certain tasks in the organism. The red blood cells (erythrocytes) transport oxygen, the nerve cells carry information, glandular cells secrete specific substances, muscle cells are responsible for body movements, and sex cells serve reproduction. The various functions of a cell are all coded for by way of specific genetic information, stored in certain sections of the DNA (desoxyribonucleic acid) of the cell itself. Pre-programmed here are processes like cell division and the synthesis of all the necessary proteins. These two processes are essential prerequi-

sites for the development of a multi-cellular organism from a fertilised ovum. It is remarkable that such diversified cells as are found in the brain, lungs, muscles, or liver, all develop from undifferentiated precursors. Cells with different functions also have different "life expectancies". Some cells last for only a few hours or days (eg intestinal epithelial cells), and others, like neural cells, live as long as the organism itself.

Number: The estimated total number of cells constituting the human body is an astonishing 100 million million (10^{14})! It is practically impossible to visualise a number like 10^{14}. To count up to this number, counting non-stop at the rate of one per second, day and night, would take three million years. The number of red corpuscles in the blood, the most numerous of all the cell types, is $25 \times 10^{12} = 25$ million million. But, unlike all other cells, they have neither a nucleus nor cellular organelles. The total number of brain cells is about ten million million.

Taking the average size of a cell as 40 µm, all the cells of a human body, placed side by side, would form a chain reaching 100 times around the equator.

DNA

– information storage technology way beyond computers

The body's most precious substance is stored deep inside the cells, in the tiny nucleus, namely the genetic information, known as the genome. If this information were to be written down using the alphabet, it would fill one thousand books, each having 1000 pages with 3,000 letters to the page. The human genome (inherited material) consists of three thousand million genetic "letters". If all these letters were typed in one line, it would extend from the North Pole to the equator. A good typist working 220 eight-hour days per year, at a typing speed of 300 letters a minute, would require 95 years for this task – much longer than her entire working life!

Taking into account the time required for planning and testing up to the implementation of the final system, a scientific programmer produces 40 symbols of program code per day on average. It would thus require a team of 8,000 programmers, devoting their entire career to this project, to program the human genome. But no human programmer knows how to structure this program and fit it into a DNA fibre measuring only one metre if stretched out. [1]

The DNA molecule. *Schematic representation of the three-dimensional double helical structure of DNA (DNA = desoxyribonucleic acid). Two polynucleotide strands are spirally wound round each other, thus forming a double helix. The base pairs, coupled by means of hydrogen bridges, are arranged in a plane perpendicular to the helical axis. Base pairs comprise either adenine with thymine, or cytosine with guanine. It follows that the molar quantity ratios are A:T = C:G = 1:1. The distance from one spiral loop to the next is 3.4 nanometres (nm), the diameter is 2 nm, and the distance between the stacked base pairs is 0.34 nm (1 nm = 10^{-9} m = one thousand millionth of a metre or 1 millionth of a millimetre).*

Storage density: The storage medium of genetic information is the double stranded DNA (chemical name: de(s)oxyribonucleic acid; see diagram on page 74). The volume [2] of human DNA is extremely small, only three thousand millionths of a cubic millimetre (3×10^{-9} mm^3). Its storage density is enormous, many magnitudes higher than the latest computer chips. In fact, it is the highest known. Let us try to visualise it:

If one could stretch out the head of a pin measuring 2 mm in diameter until it became a thread having the same thickness as a DNA molecule, it would be 33 times as long as the equator! Could you have imagined that?

If the genome information were in printed form, it would require 12,000 paperbacks of 160 pages each. Compared to the current 16 Megabit computer chips, a human DNA strand stores an amazing 1,400 times as much information.

To get a further idea of the almost unimaginable density of information in the DNA molecule, imagine you had just enough DNA to fit into a pinhead. Now imagine the information contained in an ordinary pocket paperback of 160 pages. How many such lots of information could you store in this tiny amount of DNA? The answer is 15×10^{12} (15 million million). If you actually had that many of these books and put them on top of one another in a pile, this would be 500 times as high as the distance (384,000 km) from the earth to the moon! To put it another way – if you distributed these books equally among the roughly 6 billion people on Earth, each person would get 2,500 copies!

[1] **Total length of the DNA strand (germ cell):**
L is equal to (the number of letters) x (the distance between letters)
= $3 \times 10^9 \times 0.34 \times 10^{-9}$ m = 1.02 m

[2] **Volume of the DNA strand (germ cell):**
$V = (\pi/4) \times (2 \times 10^{-9} \text{ m})^2 \times 1.02 \text{ m} = 3.2 \times 10^{-18} \text{ m}^3$
= 3.2×10^{-9} mm^3 = 3.2 μm^3
1 m^3 (cubic metre) = 10^9 mm^3 (cubic millimetres)
1 mm^3 = 10^9 μm^3 (cubic micrometres)

Structure: The total amount of genetic information can be compared to a library, where single books represent chromosomes, and their chapters are the genes. Genes are like entries in a gigantic encyclopedia. There are 23 pairs of chromosomes in the nuclei of our somatic (body) cells, making up the diploid (Greek *diplóos* = double) number of 46 chromosomes. Single chromosomes can be distinguished according to their total length, the length of the chromosomal arms, and the position of the centromere, the point at which they are constricted. With the exception of the sex chromosomes, the chromosomes from each parent correspond to those from the other parent in regard to the type and sequence of the hereditary characteristics. Women have two equal sized sex chromosomes (XX), but men have a larger and a smaller sex chromosome (XY).

The 23 human chromosome pairs comprise a double complement of approximately 100,000 inherited characteristics or genes. Every gene occurs twice, one derived from the mother, and the other from the father; they are thus known as diploid chromosomes. In contrast to the body cells, the germ cells (egg and sperm cells) have a single complement of chromosomes, called haploid (Greek *haplous* = single). Since the 100,000 genes are shared among 23 chromosomes, each chromosome is made up of about 4,400 genes.

The DNA molecules of bacteria, when stretched out, are around one millimetre long. This corresponds to around 3×10^6 nucleotide pairs. The well known bacterium E. Coli has 7.3×10^6 nucleotide pairs. In human body cells the total length of the DNA is around 2 metres, about 6×10^9 nucleotide pairs.

We must distinguish between the gametes or sex cells (which carry the information of heredity to the next generation) and the somatic or body cells. In the gametes (sperm and egg cells) the total length of the DNA threads is around 1 m, divided into 23 chromosomes. That represents 3×10^9 nucleotide pairs. These can constitute 10^9 words (triplets, each of three chemical letters). The nucleotides are the four chemical letters of the genetic alphabet, called Adenine, Guanine, Cytosine and Thymine. Human body cells carry a dual batch of hereditary information – one from the father and one from the mother. So they have $2 \times 23 = 46$ chromosomes, corresponding to a DNA length of 2 metres (6×10^9 nucleotide pairs).

The number of possible genes can be estimated. We start with an average sized gene product (protein), and look at the number of DNA building blocks (nucleotides) needed to code for that number of amino acids. For example, human hemoglobin, the pigment in red blood cells. The alpha chain has 141, the beta chain 146 amino acids. Each amino acid needs three nucleotides to code for it, so that means for both chains we need $3 \times (141+146) = 861$ nucleotide pairs. Therefore our DNA should theoretically be able to code for $3 \times 10^9/861$ genes coding for proteins the size of hemoglobin. In reality, however, the majority of the DNA consists of sequences which do not code for proteins, and their function is still unclear today (though some hints may be gradually emerging). Only 50,000 to 100,000 genes actually code for proteins. To put it another way: Only about three percent of the genome actually codes for proteins such as insulin or hemoglobin. Such program codes are identical for all people. Remarkably, in most instances, more than one gene codes for a given characteristic (e. g. eye colour).

It seems necessary to assume that in addition to its protein coding portions, DNA contains countless additional levels of structure and function. Such stored information concepts are just as much required to code for the development of the smallest organelles such as the mitochondria and ribosomes, as for building the large organs (e. g. heart, kidneys, brain) and the overall integrated organism. As yet, no one has been able to decode this incredibly complex system. Perhaps some light will be shed on this by research over the next few years.

If the total paternal contribution to heredity is contained in a sperm cell, and the maternal in an egg, then this would have to not just involve the total anatomy and physiology of a human being, but also our numerous predispositions and gifts. For example, musical ability, aggressiveness, or language aptitude. Are the non-material characteristics of people, for example, the ability to love, or experience joy, in fact reducible to being described by a nucleotide sequence? Here we still face major scientific mysteries.

Information processing: Our 100,000 genes provide exact instructions to each cell for manufacturing everything required for it to carry out the role for which it is programmed; whether hormones, enzymes, mucus, sebum, the weapons of the immune system, or the impulses in the nerve cells of the central nervous system.

One might well ask at this point: How is this information decoded, and how are these abstract "words" translated into concrete protein molecules? This never-ending process takes place inside an unimaginably small space, namely within the cells, each measuring only a few hundredths of a millimetre. Special protein molecules locate a particular piece of information – a gene – copy it, and prepare a messenger, a chemical relative of DNA called messenger-RNA. This mRNA then travels from the control centre in the nucleus out into the cytoplasm, to the ribosomes. These small granular bodies are where protein synthesis takes place. When these RNA messengers arrive here, they specify the sequence in which the 20 types of amino acids, the building blocks of all proteins, are to be assembled. Protein molecules are constructed here "block by block", just as a house is built brick by brick; they are subsequently dispatched to carry out their various vital functions.

The next important step, namely the formation of specific structures like cells and organs from these protein molecules, is very complex, and is not yet fully understood. But we do know that it is somehow encoded in our genes', and it largely determines what we are. Our genes ensure that we become human beings rather than animals. Our gender, the colour of our eyes, skin and hair, and to a great extent our size, are all determined by our personal genome. It sets parameters for

our intelligence and, to a large extent, determines our never-to-be-repeated unique personality. All these patterns are set at the precise moment in which the male chromosomes in a sperm cell meet up with those of a female egg cell (ovum). The moment of fertilisation truly is the starting point of our life.

A comparison: Each of our approximately 100 million million (10^{14}) cells has the following main components: a cell membrane, many pores and channels in this membrane, many mitochondria for regulating the flow of energy, many ribosomes which translate genetic information into proteins, and a nucleus containing the genetic information in the form of DNA.

Nowadays many people are familiar with the parts of a personal computer (PC), like hard disk, read/write head, interface, and network card. To explain the performance and complex functioning of a biological cell, Zoltán Takács, a biophysicist, compared the processing and storage of information in a cell with what happens inside a computer. If a cell in simplified form is regarded as a computer, we have the following analogies:

– The cell membrane would be the computer housing, but it is only 10 nanometres thick (= one hundred thousandth of a millimetre).
– The pores and channels are the interfaces.
– The mitochondria comprise 800 network cards.
– A ribosome would be a central processing unit (CPU), but a biological cell has more than six million CPUs.
– The nucleus would correspond to a hard drive. There would then be 23 different hard disks (= chromosomes), each of which has its own backup disk. The storage capacities of these 23 disks add up to about 1 Gigabyte. Biological "hard disks" are actually not hard, but can perhaps be regarded more like "floppy disks"; the 46 strands of DNA do not rotate around a fixed spindle, but occur as loose clusters in the nucleus.
– The diameter of this biological computer is about 20 micrometres (= two hundredths of a millimetre).

It is obvious from even this small number of facts about "biological computers" that, next to the comparatively simple computers of our own technology, they are masterpieces of miniaturisation, complexity, and design perfection.

All cells in our body carry the same information, regardless of their locality (e. g. kidney, liver, or arm). But different cell types access and process different sections of the available information. As in the case of physical computers, the original information is not transferred to the CPUs. Copies are made and transported. In a computer the read/write head is positioned at the beginning of an application program on the hard disk to copy it. But in a cell several reading heads begin at different locations to make copies simultaneously, so that the various pieces of information required for a certain type of cell are read from all the "hard disks" at the same time. A biological computer performs two kinds of "computations": It provides the information for protein synthesis as described above, and it replicates itself by means of cell division.

The genome project: Scientists from all over the world instigated an ambitious 15 year project to chart the human genetic code and to decipher it letter by letter (known as sequencing). For this purpose the "Human Genome Organisation", which has about 900 members in 40 countries, was officially commenced on 1 October 1990. The effort required to determine the letter sequence of human DNA, was originally estimated as many thousands of man-years. We have already given you some idea of the enormous amount of information in the entire sequence. It is assumed that only about three percent of this huge amount of information represents the approximately 100,000 human genes, distributed among 23 chromosomes. The purpose of the other 97 % is still largely unknown.

The structure of the DNA molecule: Chemically and structurally the DNA molecule is one of the most complex and versatile of molecules, a necessity in view of all its functions. This versatility is necessary to provide for all its functions. It looks like a double helix from the outside (Greek

hélix = spiral) comprising two intertwined spiral strands. Each strand is a long molecular chain, and the two strands are essentially parallel, intertwined in a right-hand spiral. The genetic code comprises four chemical letters adenine (A), guanine (G), thymine (T), and cytosine (C). Many genes do not consist of a continuous piece of DNA, but are made up like a mosaic of several separated segments.

In all cells, the genetic information stored in the DNA molecules controls protein synthesis, and another nucleic acid, ribonucleic acid (RNA), handles the transfer of all the information. In general, all cells of an organism contain identical DNA molecules, but not all genes are active at the same time in all the cells.

Proteins: Proteins are the workhorses of life. If we regard the DNA molecule as the blueprint of life, then the many different kinds of proteins are not only the bricks and mortar, they make up the required tools as well as some of them being the manual labourers which perform the actual construction jobs. Our genes provide the conceptual foundations (they store the "software"), but we are what we are (the "hardware") because of our proteins. Both DNA molecules and proteins consist of long chains made up of strings of subunits, but their functions are fundamentally different. DNA molecules comprise the genetic archives. On the other hand, proteins exhibit an unimaginable diversity of three-dimensional shapes, reflecting their multiplicity of functions. Some of the tasks of proteins are that they serve as structural elements for the body, as messenger molecules, as receptors for messengers, as individual cell identifiers, and as substances defending against cells bearing foreign identifiers. Probably the most important proteins are the enzymes, which control the rate of biochemical processes by acting as catalysts. Certain enzymes can accelerate some reactions a millionfold or even more. Enzymes are also indispensable for the actual process of converting genetic information into its resultant products and processes.

Structure and chemistry of proteins: Although there are many amino acids, the Creator chose

78

only 20 of them from which to construct all conceivable proteins (and thereby the structures) necessary for life. In the genetic code, three letters specify one amino acid, and every protein consists of an exactly determined sequence of amino acids. All the physical and chemical properties of an individual protein are determined by the length of the chain and the specific sequence of amino acids. The spatial disposition or folding of the chain is especially important. Proteins fold in such a way that the free energy is kept to a minimum; this means that a protein assumes the most "comfortable" shape. In principle one can only deduce the three-dimensional structure of a protein from the amino acid sequence, if all the forces acting on all of its thousands of atoms are known, as well as their effects on the surrounding molecules of the solvent. Such calculations are impossible in the present state of our knowledge, even using the most powerful computer systems**. But when the Creator made all living organisms, He constructed each and every protein in such a way that all the desired properties were obtained.

* With a possible inherited (maternal) contribution from the cytoplasmic structure of the egg cell.

** Remarkably, it now appears that the folding of many proteins after their construction (which would often be too slow if left to the physical forces acting on a particular protein's components) is aided by specially tailored "chaperone" molecules.

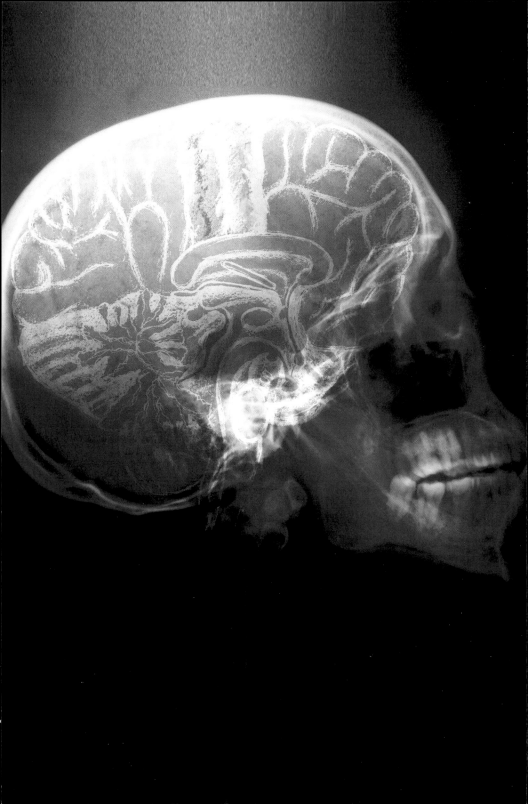

The brain

– the most complex structure in the universe

"For thousands of years people have tried to understand the brain. The ancient Greeks thought it was like a radiator to cool the blood. In this century it has been compared to a switchboard, a computer, and a hologram – and no doubt it will be likened to any number of machines yet to be invented. But none of these analogues is adequate, for the brain is unique in the universe and unlike anything men have ever made."
(Robert Ornstein / Richard F Thompson: *The Amazing Brain*. Houghton Miffin Company, Boston, 1984)

The human brain, located inside our skull and weighing about 1.5 kg, is described by professors Robert Ornstein (University of California) and Richard F. Thompson (Stanford University) in the above words. It can rightly be called the most complex physical structure in the universe.

The brain is the central controlling organ of our nervous system. It controls, watches over, and coordinates nearly all the processes occurring in the body. It collects, evaluates and stores sensory impressions, and effects meaningful responses.

Practically nothing is known about the way information processing actually takes place in the brain. Nobody knows how the perceived semantic information is derived from the incoming electrical signals. We do know that certain activities originate in the cerebral cortex (the outer layer of the cerebrum), and we also know that certain memories are stored there. But we do not know how they are stored, nor how we recall specific memories. We also do not know how novel ideas originate, nor what happens in the brain when something new is learnt. The little we do know about the functions of various parts of the brain has essentially been obtained by observing the changes resulting from brain damage or tumours. The only real knowledge we have of the brain is on the statistical level, like the number of structural elements and the estimated number of interconnections. Even this statistical information highlights the astounding properties of the most complex structure in the universe.

The number of structural units: The brain comprises about one hundred thousand million nerve cells (100×10^9). The term "neurons" coined by W. von Waldeyer in 1891, is used as a synonym for nerve cells. They are the structural elements of the brain, and their number is of the same magnitude as the number of stars in our local galaxy. No two of them have exactly the same shape. In addition to this immense number of neurons, there are also one hundred thousand million other cells, providing metabolic functions and structural support.

Every neuron is connected to thousands of others by means of synapses (Greek *synapsis* = connection). Even though each nerve cell is not in direct contact with every other one, it is indirectly linked with all others via intermediate connections. It follows that the number of possible pathways linking the nerve cells in every human brain is extremly large: 5×10^{21} (= 5,000 million million million). It would require 40 printed pages simply to list the number of direct connections of a single neuron. In order to list all direct neuronal links, 40 pages times the number of neurons = 4000×10^9 pages, would be required.

Assuming that one book comprises 400 pages, the required number of books would be $4000 \times 10^9 / 400 = 10 \times 10^9$. This result is breathtakingly large. Such a list would require a library containing ten thousand million books of 400 pages. The largest library in the world, namely the Library of Congress in Washington, contains about 20 million volumes. This means that we would require 500 such libraries just to list the direct connections in the human brain!

The number of synapses is thus appreciably greater than the number of neurons. One neuron receives information from several hundreds, up to thousands, of other neurons, and transmits it to a similar number of other nerve cells.

Neurons are the building blocks of the brain. They possess the same genes as other body cells, they are constructed along similar lines, and they are kept alive by the same biochemical processes which support other cells. But they differ in some essential aspects, making them the most extraordinary cells in a living organism. The differences include shape, type of cell membrane, and the presence of a structure known as a synapse. The cell membrane has the ability to produce neural signals, and in the synapses these signals are carried to other nerve cells by means of transfer substances called neurotransmitters.

During the development of the organism from a fertilised ovum, neurons are formed at the astounding rate of 250,000 per minute over nine months. It used to be thought that neurons do not subdivide after an embryo is fully developed. Thus, the number of nerve cells formed up to the moment of birth had to last one's entire lifetime. Recent evidence indicates that at least some nerve cells may be replaced in the adult organism after all.

With between ten and fifty thousand connections per nerve cell, the entire system forms an immeasurably complex branched network. If it were possible to describe it as a circuit diagram, then even if each neuron were represented by a single pinhead, such a circuit diagram would require an area of several square kilometres! Compare this to the complex engineering drawings which are often produced according to the DIN-A0-Format on only one square metre (841 mm x 1189 mm). Such a circuit diagram of the brain would be several hundred times more complex than the entire global telephone network. In reality, nobody really knows anything much about the internal connections of the brain.

The total length of the nerve fibres in the greater brain (cerebrum) is about 500,000 km, with some authors even estimating it to be as much as one million km. Our "command centre", the brain, would be useless if there were no links to the body. Outside of the brain the total length of nerve fibres is 380,000 km, which is equal to the distance of the moon from the earth. They form a branching network throughout the body, continually carrying information and commands to

and fro between the brain and all our other parts. In places the thickness of these fibres is only one thousandth of a millimetre, but messages travel along them at a speed of about 40 metres per second or 144 km/h. This is equal to the speed of a hurricane-force wind (force 12).

Processing speed: The incredibly dense neuronal network can process signals at a very high rate. The brain can do 10^{18} = 1 million million million computations in a second, which is a hundred million times as fast as the fastest super computer at time of writing (10^{10} calculations per second). The most fascinating aspect, however, is not the actual physical performance of the brain, but its ability to process these unimaginably vast quantities of information in unique ways which we cannot yet fully comprehend.

Energy consumption: The brains of dogs and cats are responsible for between five and six per cent of the energy consumption of the entire animal. This is more or less true for all mammals (regardless of body size), with the exception of primates (apes, monkeys, etc.). In rhesus monkeys, the percentage is about nine, but for humans it is an impressive 20 per cent. Our brain requires about 20 Watts, which is one fifth of the energy (100 Watts) consumed by the whole body. The brain of a growing embryo requires a much greater proportion of energy, namely 60 per cent.

Structure: The cerebrum occupies the greater part of the brain's volume. It consists of two halves or hemispheres, each of which is responsible for the functioning of the opposite half of the body. The two halves are connected via the corpus callosum, which is essentially a broad cable made up of 300 million nerve fibres. Each hemisphere is covered by a three millimetre thick layer of nerve cells. This layer, the cerebral cortex, is intensely convoluted and has a total surface area of about 2,200 cm². The cortex [1] enables us to organise, to remember, to understand, to com-

---

[1] **Cortex:** Latin *cortex* = bark, crust, shell. The word cortex is used anatomically to indicate the outer layer or surface of an organ. In the brain there is the cerebral cortex, and the cerebellar cortex; the kidneys have the renal cortex.

1. Corpus callosum
2. Anterior commissure
3. Thalamus with anterior nucleus
4. Olfactory bulb with olfactory nerves
5. Optic chiasma
6. Pituitary gland
7. Pons
8. Spinal medulla
9. Medulla oblongata
10. Cerebellum
11. Pineal body
12. Great cerebral vein
13. Sensory cortex
14. Central sulcus
15. Motor cortex

Vertical section through the brain

83

municate, to evaluate, and to be creative and inventive.

Between the brain stem and the cortex are various structures which play a major part in the regulation of such things as body temperature, blood pressure, pulse rate, blood sugar and electrolyte levels, among others. The hypothalamus and the pituitary gland play an important role in this system. The former can be regarded as the "brain" of the brain. The size of a pea and weighing only about four grams, it is the most complex and amazing part of the brain. It controls eating, drinking, sleeping, alertness, body temperature, the equilibrium of many physiological processes, pulse rate, hormones, and sexuality. It also controls the most important gland in the brain, namely the pituitary gland, by means of a combination of electrical and chemical messages. The pituitary in turn controls many body functions through hormones, which are chemical substances carried by the blood to specific target cells. The targets of the pituitary's hormones are often other hormone-secreting glands (e.g. the thyroid and adrenal glands). The pituitary acts somewhat like a hormone symphony conductor, regulating the 'instruments' which regulate other functions.

Information storage: At the cellular level, there are basically two kinds of information storage. One type is the unimaginably large quantity of genetic information contained in the DNA molecules of all cells. The second kind of storage takes place in the brain, which also involves an enormous amount of information. In the first of these, the amount of (genetic) information is fixed at conception. The second type occurs through experience and learning. Each of us acquires an ever-increasing amount of mentally stored information throughout our lifetime. Every person's uniqueness is not least to do with their mind, in which the memories, events and experiences of a lifetime are stored. Our ability to learn, which varies between individuals, obviously depends on properties of the complex cerebral network. These properties themselves are undoubtedly determined to a great extent by our genes.

The entire vocabulary of all languages we have mastered, as well as their complete grammatical structures, are stored in our brain, enabling us to freely and flexibly use language. The storage of visual images is unique in the way these memories may be recalled clearly at any time. An important additional aspect of that which makes us human is our ability to imagine and to fantasise, both of which somehow involve the brain.

Memory/Mind: Memory is the ability to store and recall mental information. Without this processing ability, we could neither see, nor hear, nor think. We would not be able to express our feelings in language, nor would we be aware of our personal identity. We would be intellectually dead biological machines.

An adult knows the meaning of between 20,000 and 100,000 words, which could be appreciably more if he/she has some knowledge of foreign languages. Living in society requires familiarity with many common customs – how to negotiate city traffic, how to buy and sell, how to use a telephone, and how to check in at a hotel. In addition, we have at our disposal a considerable amount of specialised knowledge gained during education, and in our professional life. During leisure times we occupy ourselves with various hobbies and recreational activities. All this information is at our mental beck and call. Consider the task of trying to construct a similar source of knowledge, just as comprehensive and able to be accessed with the same blindingly fast precision. We begin to catch a mere glimpse of just how amazing and fascinating our mind really is.

Just consider the following questions: Did Archimedes have hands? Did Harrison Ford participate in the Boer War? What was Bach's telephone number?

If our brain were merely a computer system with a large hard disk that could only access a store of previously learned information, then the above three questions could only be answered with "I don't know". But we possess the crucial (and underrated) ability of deductive thought (see also the chapter "Like God, we can think").

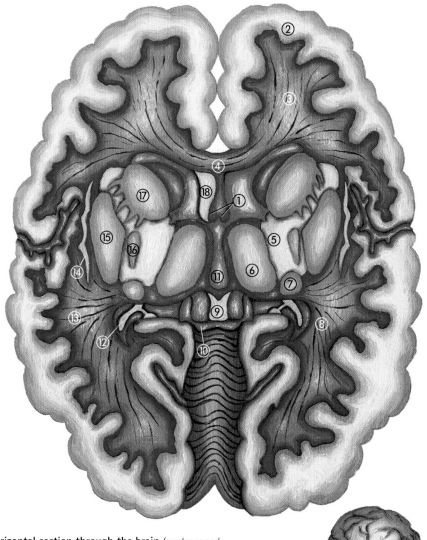

Horizontal section through the brain *(cerebrum and cerebellum). The plane of section is shown in the inset (b).*

b)

① Fornix
② Grey matter of the cerebral cortex
③ White matter of the medulla
④ Corpus callosum
⑤ Geniculate body
⑥ Thalamus
⑦ Optic chiasma
⑧ Optic radiation
⑨ Pineal gland
⑩ Lamina quadrigemina
⑪ Third ventricle
⑫ Posterior horn of the lateral ventricle
⑬ Auditory radiation
⑭ Claustrum
⑮ Lentiform nucleus
⑯ Globus pallidus
⑰ Head of the caudate nucleus
⑱ Anterior horn of the lateral ventricle

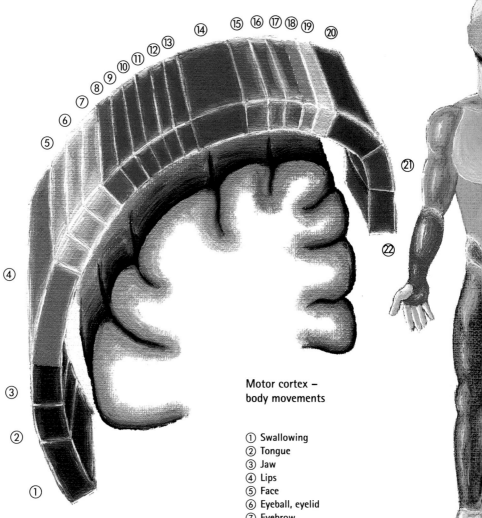

**Motor cortex –
body movements**

1. Swallowing
2. Tongue
3. Jaw
4. Lips
5. Face
6. Eyeball, eyelid
7. Eyebrow
8. Neck
9. Thumbs
10. Index finger
11. Middle finger
12. Ring finger
13. Little finger
14. Hand
15. Wrist
16. Elbow
17. Shoulder
18. Torso
19. Hip
20. Knee
21. Ankle
22. Toes

The motor and sensory cortex, indicating the representation of body regions. Note that those parts of the body where the muscles have to carry out more differentiated actions are represented by relatively large cortical areas. For example, the area occupied by nerve cells supplying the hand is exceptionally large. This is because a large number of neurons is required for such delicate and complex movements as violin-playing, writing, or performing a delicate surgical operation.

⑤ ⑥ ⑦ ⑧   ⑨   ⑩   ⑪   ⑫   ⑬   ⑭ ⑮ ⑯ ⑰ ⑱ ⑲   ⑳   ㉑   ④   ③   ②   ①   ㉒   ㉓   ㉔   ㉕

Sensory cortex –
bodily sensation

① Genitalia
② Toes
③ Foot
④ Leg
⑤ Hip
⑥ Torso
⑦ Neck
⑧ Head
⑨ Shoulder, arm, elbow
⑩ Forearm
⑪ Wrist
⑫ Hand
⑬ Little finger
⑭ Ring finger
⑮ Middle finger
⑯ Index finger
⑰ Thumb
⑱ Eye
⑲ Nose
⑳ Face
㉑ Lips
㉒ Teeth, gums, jaw
㉓ Tongue
㉔ Throat
㉕ Abdominal cavity

87

The fact that Archimedes had hands has never been stored anywhere in our brain, but we can immediately answer this question in the affirmative. We deduce that if he did not have hands, this fact would have been common knowledge. In regard to the second question, there may be many unknown men involved in the Boer War, but from the fact that the well-known actor Harrison Ford was born well after it ended, we can deduce that he definitely did not take part in it. And what about Johann Sebastian Bach's (1685 – 1750) telephone number? A computer would search through long lists of phone numbers, and then report that this composer either did not have a telephone, or that his name had not yet been entered. But we know when the telephone was invented, so we can quickly conclude that he could have had neither telephone nor phone number.

Interpretation instead of mere data acquisition: Our senses carry a million times more information to the brain than it is able to consciously process. And the brain does not merely register the observed realities around us like a camera or a tape recorder. Our brain reduces the flood of external data signals, simultaneously interpreting them and constructing a very personal inner world. This internally created reality is generally quite distinct from the outside world. A red rose is actually a physical structure which reflects light of a specific wavelength. Only in our brain is there such a thing as the colour red, along with the knowledge that this structure is a flower. Our brain compares these signals from outside with what it has already stored about roses previously seen. At the same time, memories of associated events and emotions are awakened. Our nerve cells not only produce an image of a rose, they evaluate it as well. An image of a red rose can cause us to recall its fragrance, and perhaps also some tender memories of a great love. All these things happen without any conscious involvement. The American neurophysiologist, Benjamin Libet, discovered that our consciousness lags about half a second behind the activities of the brain. By the time we are conscious of making a decision about something, our brain has long since analysed and evaluated all the information from our surroundings relevant to that situation.

Up to now we have ascribed all mental properties to the brain's physical make-up alone. But in the next chapter it will be shown that such a view is not really adequate to encompass all its functions.

In spite of many research findings, the brain is still mostly like a vast blank "unknown territory" on our map of scientific knowledge.

Some quotations by scientists researching the human brain:

"The more precisely neuro-scientists try to describe the functioning of our brain, the clearer it becomes that all their measurements and models do not encompass the central aspect of consciousness, namely the subjective appreciation of qualities like colour and scent, a moment of reflection, or an emotion."
(David J Chalmers: The puzzle of conscious perception, *Spektrum der Wissenschaft*, Feb 1996, page 40)

"At the present stage, with a reasonable start in understanding the structure and workings of individual cells, neurobiologists are in the position of a man who knows something about the physics of resistors, condensators and transistors and who looks inside a television set. He cannot begin to understand how the machine works as a whole until he learns how the elements are wired together and until he has at least some idea of the purpose of the machine, of its subassemblies and of their interactions. In brain research the first step beyond the individual neuron and its workings is to learn how the larger subunits of the brain are interconnected and how each unit is built up."
(David H Hubel: *The Brain. Scientific American*, Vol. 241, No. 3, Sept. 1979, p. 44)

"After thousands of scientists have studied the brain for centuries, the only adequate way to describe it is as a miracle."
(Robert Ornstein / Richard F. Thompson: *Our brain – a living labyrinth*. Houghton Miffin Company, Boston, 1984)

Body, soul, and spirit

– man is more than just matter

At this stage the reader might be under the impression that man might be a very complex structure, but in the final analysis we are nothing more than matter. In fact, there is a philosophical view called materialism in which man is regarded as just that: nothing more than a collection of material substances. This concept is just one of several so-called monistic worldviews.

Monism (Greek *mónos* = sole, single) denotes a doctrine of one-ness. A German philosopher, Christian Wolff (1679 - 1754) introduced this concept. According to the strict monistic view there are no separate realms of being; it attempts to explain everything via a single unifying principle. For example, the belief that everything that exists is God. Materialism, which denies the existence of any God or supernatural realm, is classified as a monistic philosophy, since all phenomena are thought to be explained in terms of one principle – i.e., the inherent properties of matter. This view is also apparent in the writings of Friedrich Engels (1820 - 1895), the co-founder of Marxism: "The material world which can be observed by our senses, to which we ourselves belong, is the only reality ... matter is not the result of mind, but mind is merely the highest product of matter."

The widely proclaimed evolutionism of our present day is also a monistic philosophical system. The basis of evolution is pure materialism, and no plan or purpose is recognised. The consequences of evolutionism have been described as follows by Carsten Bresch, a geneticist of Freiburg (Germany): "Nature seems to be a purposeless and meaningless machine. Have we paid for our new intellectual freedom by relinquishing the meaning of our existence? Half-knowing man stands alone, uprooted in the limitless expanse of an icy universe – lost in the chain of generations. He came from nothing – and is going nowhere.

What is the purpose of it all?" (from "Zwischenstufe Leben – Evolution ohne Ziel?"; "Life as transition – evolution without purpose?").

It should be obvious that monism is unable to explain life in all its diverse manifestations. Taking the human brain as an example, Sir John C. Eccles (1903 -), an Australian Nobel Laureate and brain researcher, rejected monism, and propounded the dualistic view of man.

Dualism: (Greek *duo* = two). According to this view reality consists of two opposite realms of being, like for example matter and mind. On the basis of his brain researches, Eccles describes

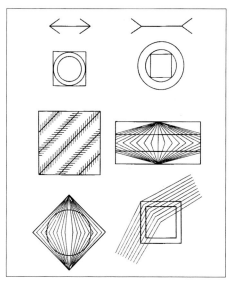

Figure 1: *Optical illusions of regular figures which have had supplementary lines added.*

man as a dualistic being. We will pursue this idea further, since he has (unintentionally!?) built a bridge to the biblical view of man.

Figure 1 contains several examples of sensory illusions. Looking at these sketches can be irritating:

- The distances between the arrow tips are equal. But the directions in which they point make them appear unequal (illusion of length).
- The second row of figures contains two equal-sized circles which nevertheless appear to be different in size (illusion of size).
- The two sets of parallel lines seem to converge or be crooked (illusion of direction).
- In the lower part of the diagram the circle as well as the square seems to be distorted (illusion of shape).

In *Figure 2* we see three men walking along a street. The person in front seems to be the tallest one, and the one in the rear the shortest. This is an illusion, since all three of them are the same height. The surrounding perspective lines make them appear to be of different sizes.

The three diagrams in *Figure 3* do not mislead our senses, but, in contrast to *Figures 1* and *2*, they confront our perception with more than one possible interpretation:

The semi-opened book can either be seen from the inside or from the outside.
The staircase can either be seen as ascending steps, or as viewed from the underside.
The cubical block is even more complex, since there are three possible ways of "seeing" it.

Figure 2: *Are these three men the same size? (Example of an optical illusion).*

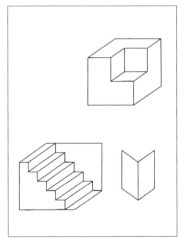

Figure 3: *Illusions of perception. Each of these three geometric figures can be interpreted in more than one way.*

Figure 4: *Young girl or old lady? (Example of an illusion of perception).*

a) A small cube lies in the corner of a room or is fixed to the ceiling.

b) A small cube is placed in front of the larger one, at one corner.

c) Similar to b), but now there is a cubical hollow in one corner of the large cube.

And what do we see in *Figure 4*? A young woman or an old one? Both are possible. This is also an example of an illusion of perception.

John Eccles draws conclusions from these. Even though a diagram can be interpreted in more than one way, we can be sure of one thing: there is only a single, unambiguous image on the reti-

na which is then electrically transmitted to the brain. Here the optical image corresponds to a precisely defined neuronal connection – whatever form that may take. From this Eccles deduces the existence of another independent entity which observes and interprets the actual brain connections. He calls this interpreter the mind (others might call this the soul).

Brain and mind can exchange information, but the mind has the freedom to interpret one specific picture in various ways. This dualism is illustrated graphically in *Figure 5* (World 1 and World 2). World 1 represents the required material part – the brain, and World 2 depicts the nonmaterial

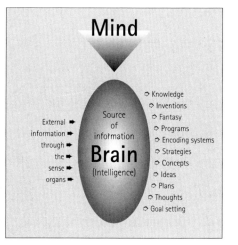

Figure 5: *The dualistic view of man. On the one side we have the material aspects (the body with all its anatomical details), and on the other side is the non-material part (the I, the self, the mind, and the will). Eccles postulates the presence of a liaison brain, which is "observed" and interpreted by the non-material part.*

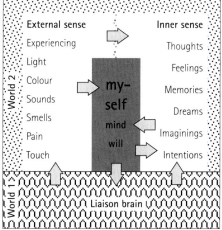

Figure 6: *The interactions between brain and mind according to the dualistic view of man.*

ORIGIN OF MAN

1. Plan

Genesis 1:26: "Let us make man..."

2. Execution

Genesis 2:7: "the Lord God ...

formed man
from the dust
of the ground

and breathed
into his nostrils
the breath of life,

Spirit
from God

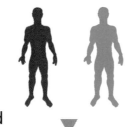

Body
from the ground

3. Result

Body – soul – spirit

and the man became a living being. "

Figure 7: *The biblical view of man. Human beings were created with a body, a soul, and a spirit.*

MAN'S STRUCTURE

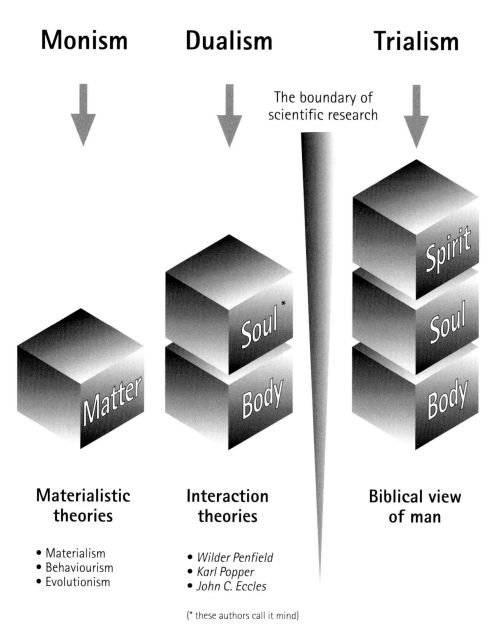

Figure 8: *The three common and strongly divergent views of man. The sources of information are fundamentally quite distinct. Monism is purely a philosophical view, dualism can be deduced from scientific research, but biblical trialism can only be known by revelation.*

aspect – the mind, which, according to Eccles, includes the I, the self, the psyche, and the will. Both components are interconnected via the external sense (experiences of which we are made conscious through our sense organs) as well as by means of the inner sense (thoughts, feelings, memories, dreams, imaginings, and intentions).

It is not hard to draw some straightforward scientific conclusions from this. The dualistic view of man, equipped with this complex organ, the brain, is graphically illustrated in *Figure 6*, which indicates both the material and nonmaterial components. It is obvious from this representation that knowledge, strategies, thoughts and purposes cannot have a material origin.

At this point, we have reached the limits of scientific research, because questions of man's origin, and destiny after death, cannot be resolved by this model. But Eccles did have some inkling of the truth when he wrote: "The components of our existence in World 2 are not of a material nature and are thus not necessarily subject to the dissolution that destroys all the World 1 components of an individual at the moment of death" (from: Eccles, Zeier*: Gehirn und Geist* [Mind and Brain], München 1980, p 190).

To know more about how man is really made up, we need to ask Him Who made human beings. For this purpose we consult the Bible, where this important question is answered on the very first page. God is the ultimate First Cause. And He created everything, as stated emphatically in Genesis 1:1: "In the beginning God created..." The purpose of this creation was human beings, as God had planned. We read in Genesis 1:26: "Let us make man..." If, like me, you have an engineering frame of mind, you will particularly appreciate God's conceptual framework for the various stages of man's creation:

1. Plan
2. Execution
3. Result

These steps are illustrated in *Figure 7*. The one verse, Genesis 2:7, is a masterpiece of concise

and exact formulation which is at the same time packed with information.

Execution: Adam was created in two phases:

In the first place God made his body from the substance of the earth. Our bodies comprise the same chemical elements as those found in the ground. It was quite a sensation when it was discovered in the 19th century that organic substances consist of the same elements as inorganic matter.

The second important component was added when God "breathed into his nostrils the breath of life". Only after this nonmaterial spirit had been infused into the physical body, did this new creation become a human being. This spirit should not be confused with the Holy Spirit. It should also be noted that the nonmaterial part, called mind by *Eccles*, is actually the soul in the biblical sense.

Result: After the two different parts, the "earthly body" and "the spirit breathed by God", had been joined, an entirely new creation came into being, namely the soul: "and the man became a living soul" (King James version). The result of this creative act of God, the joining of two different worlds, is illustrated in *Figure 7*. When these two completely different components are joined, the result of this union is the soul. The word "soul" as used in the Bible, has two meanings. It includes the entire human being, and it also describes one of the three components: body, soul, and spirit (1 Thess 5:23). This triadic combination describes man's total reality. We exist because God willed it so. He planned it, and carried out His plan purposefully.

Trialism: In light of the above biblical affirmations, it should be obvious that Eccles' dualism, although an improvement on monism, is still inadequate for a complete understanding of human beings. Because the Bible mentions three distinct human components, we introduce the concept of trialism (Greek *tri* = three) *(Figure 8)*. The fact that the joining of two components may give rise to a third and new phenomenon, can be explained in terms of a technological analogue: When an electrical current (considered as being spirit) flows though a lamp (representing the body), a third entity is produced, namely light (the phenomenon of a new soul).

Man's fall into sin: Without the trialistic biblical view of man, some fundamental biblical concepts would remain a mystery. In the garden of Eden God gave a single commandment: "You are free to eat from any tree in the garden, but you must not eat from the tree of the knowledge of good and evil, for when you eat of it, you will surely die" (Gen 2:16-17). After they had sinned, Adam and Eve still lived on, but their spirit which was in direct communication with God, died immediately. The close communion with God ended, and as a result of their sin, physical, bodily death entered the world – "the wages of sin is death" (Rom 6:23). They not only died spiritually that day, they began to die physically from then on. The end result is that eternal death awaits every person, but that does not mean that his/her existence will be ended (Luke 16:19-31). It means that man will for all eternity be separated from God. God's wrath remains on him, since "the result of one trespass was condemnation for all men" (Rom 5:18).

Salvation: But, praise God! He has provided everything necessary to make it possible for us to leave the train of death in which all of us are travelling towards eternal doom. How this happens, how our dead spirits can be revived, is discussed fully in the second part of this book.

Part 2

What is man?

Having learned of the many astonishing details of our body discussed in Part 1, there is no doubt that a human being is a masterpiece of design and construction. It would thus be foolish to assume that we developed from matter by means of blind material processes. Since the beginning the burning question has been: What is man? If we deny the fact of creation, we stumble around in the undergrowth of evolutionary thought systems without getting to the truth. When considering the works of the Creator, one inevitably must infer that He exists, since "God's invisible qualities ... have been clearly seen, being understood from what has been made" (Rom 1:20). It follows directly from His works that God exists.

But what about the other source of information, the Bible? Can we believe everything written there? Notwithstanding widely held opinions, the Bible is not merely an ancient collection of human ideas gathered over a time span of 1,500 years. On the contrary, God used about 45 people whom He selected to transmit His thoughts to us: "All Scripture is God-breathed and is useful for teaching, rebuking, correcting and training in righteousness" (2 Tim 3:16). This assertion is underlined by Peter in 2 Peter 1:21: "For prophecy never had its origin in the will of man, but men spoke from God as they were carried along by the Holy Spirit."

When Jesus prayed to his Father, He also confirmed: "Your word is truth" (John 17:17), and Paul stated "I believe everything ... that is written in the Prophets" (Acts 24:14). We base our further deliberations on these fundamental assertions which affirm the truth of all biblical statements. (Two other books by the present author deal more fully with the veracity of the Bible, namely *So steht's geschrieben* (*It is written*); [Hänssler-Verlag, Neuhausen], and *Questions I have always wanted to ask* [CLV, Bielefeld]).

The Bible is the only source which describes and encompasses all aspects of humanity. In the very first chapter we read that we were created in the image of God.

Man: The image of God?

1 The creation of man was based on a pre-conceived plan: "Let us make man in our image, in our likeness, and let them rule over the fish of the sea and the birds of the air, over the livestock, over all the earth, and over all the creatures that move along the ground" (Gen 1:26).

The plan was immediately implemented:

"So God created man in his own image, in the image of God He created him; male and female He created them" (Gen 1:27).

This plan entailed and established several facts, namely:

– This plan was implemented after all the animals had been created. Man was thus a distinctly new creature, not related in any way to the animal kingdom, despite all evolutionary ideas in this regard.

– Not only God the Father was involved in this creative act, but also the Son and the Holy Spirit, as indicated by the plural form.

– Man was made to rule over the (physical) creation. He is its regent, having been given the responsibility of its upkeep. His task is to care for all of creation.

What does it mean, to state that man was made in the image of God? God created man according to His own ideas and thoughts, in His likeness, reflecting God's own properties and qualities. We were made for communing with God and with our beloved spouse. We bear God's seal and His handwriting, as it were; we were made to serve and love God and our partner in marriage. We are meant to reproduce further copies of God's image.

God has provided us with exceptional abilities found nowhere else in the universe, to remind us of our Creator. This concept is clearly expressed in Psalm 8:5: "You made him a little lower than the heavenly beings, and crowned him with glory and honour." We were created for the purpose of being the image of God – similar to Him!

2 Each and every person is a unique image of God: God did not merely create humankind in general, but He carefully made each individual with his/her distinctive external and internal characteristics. All of us can be distinguished by date of birth, size, weight, skin-, eye- and hair colour, plus very many other details. I am so unique that I cannot cross a border with somebody else's passport. My cares and joys, my ideas, thoughts and feelings are so unique that nobody else in the whole world is like me. The German historian Leopold Ranke (1795 – 1886) asserted: "Every person is a separate thought of God."

3 Who is our Creator? The New Testament provides further insights to creation by describing the person of the Creator: "In the beginning was the Word (Greek: *the Logos*), and the Word was with God, and the Word was God. He was with God in the beginning. Through him all things were made; without him nothing was made that has been made" (John 1:1-3).

Who or what is this Word? At this point it is not yet clear. But we are given to understand that absolutely nothing in the entire universe is excluded from this act of creation, not the earth, nor the tiniest blade of grass, nor man. This secret is partially decoded in verse 10. We are told that it was a person who once resided on this our earth: "He was in the world, and … the world was made through him." But who is "He"? The full revelation is given in verse 14: "The Word became flesh and made his dwelling among us. We have seen his glory, the glory of the One and Only, who came from the Father, full of grace and truth." It follows that the Son of God, Jesus Christ, is our

Creator. "His Son, whom he appointed heir of all things, and through whom he made the universe" (Hebr 1:2). In Colossians 1:16-17 Jesus' creative activities are taken a step further, including the as yet for us invisible world:

"By him (Jesus) all things were created: things in heaven and on earth, visible and invisible, whether thrones or powers or rulers or authorities; all things were created by him and for him. He is before all things, and in him all things hold together."

The question of our origin has now been answered completely and finally: Jesus Christ is our Creator! For many readers this may come as a surprise, but it is the unequivocal teaching of the New Testament. Consequently, any idea about man's origin that does not mention nor acknowledge this Creator, is intrinsically false.

After man's sin, which will be discussed more fully in later chapters, he became separated from his Creator. At the same time many characteristics of God's image were lost. Only Christ still represents the complete image of God, as asserted in the following three quotations from the New Testament:

"He is the image of the invisible God, the first-born over all creation" (Col 1:15). "Christ … is the image of God" (2 Cor 4:4). "The Son is the radiance of God's glory and the exact representation of his being" (Hebr 1:3).

In spite of the heavy losses sustained through man's fall into sin, an appreciable fraction of the original image, derived from God, has survived the separation. All God's attributes are complete and present in the highest degree in Him; we were also intended to have His attributes, albeit at a level which is a "little lower" (Ps 8:5). This is summarised in the following ten aspects:

Like God, we can speak

God is a speaking God: "And God said" appears ten times in the creation account. We read in

Genesis 1:28: "God blessed them and said to them." God spoke to Adam and Eve. Man is addressed by God, and is called to respond. No animal can speak! Only two exceptions are mentioned in the Bible, the serpent in the garden of Eden, and Balaam's ass. But both of these animals were controlled externally; the serpent by the devil, and the donkey by God.

Only man has the gift of speech, a characteristic otherwise only possessed by God. This separates us clearly from the animal kingdom. We are able to use words creatively, but we are unable to create anything by speaking, as God can do. Our words can bless and benefit other people, but they can also be destructive. We are able to express all our feelings in words, and we can enter into trusting relationships like no other beings on Earth. In addition to the necessary "software" for speech, we have also been provided with the required "hardware":

The morphological conditions for speech are not located in a single organ. We require a voicebox (larynx) for producing sounds, a suitably shaped throat and mouth working together with the tongue, as well as a highly complex control system (the brain), all functionally coordinated with each other. If only one of them is missing, speech is impossible. In the Middle Ages, peoples' tongues were cut out to prevent them from talking. The sounds produced by the vocal cords travel upwards and are shaped in the throat and mouth to form specific phonemes (speech sounds). This requires movements of the tongue, fine-tuned with those of the lips. In addition, various resonant passages of the oral cavity contribute to the formation of understandable sounds. Each and every one of the 600 possible sounds occurring in the different human languages requires precise movements and exactly shaped tongue positions. In 1756 Johann Peter Süßmilch (1707 – 1767) established that man could not have invented speech without the required mental abilities, and, conversely, that thought in its turn depends on the previous existence of speech. The only possible solution for this paradox is that God has given man the ability to speak.

Characteristics of human speech:

- We can create new words and can link as many discrete phonemes together as we like, producing acceptable new sentences.
- We are able to construct sentences which we have never before uttered.
- We can understand sentences which we have never heard beforehand.
- An unlimited number of thoughts can be expressed in human speech.

Systems used for communication among animals are fixed and limited. No creative communion is possible, and only severely limited concepts can be expressed (for example food, danger, and sexual attraction). These cannot be compared to speech.

Like God, we can think

God is the source of all thought. No one advised Him, since wisdom originates with Him: "Oh, the depth of the riches of the wisdom and knowledge of God! How unsearchable his judgments, and his paths beyond tracing out! 'Who has known the mind of the Lord? Or who has been his counselor?' " (Rom 11:33-34).

God compares his thoughts with ours in Isaiah 55:8-9: " 'For my thoughts are not your thoughts, neither are your ways my ways', declares the Lord. 'As the heavens are higher than the earth, so are my ways higher than your ways and my thoughts than your thoughts.'"

However, despite this enormous distance from God, we too can think, consider, and contemplate. We are able to ponder fundamental issues such as life, death and wisdom, as stated in Psalm 90:12: "Teach us to number our days aright, that we may gain a heart of wisdom."

We have the ability to handle widely differing categories of thought, like inferential logic, causality and complementarity. The following ability is very important in our daily lives and in all sciences:

Deductive logic: This is the formal logical process of coming to a particular conclusion from general premises. For example: "If A, and B, (the premises) then C (the conclusion)". This conclusion is a new statement, deduced solely by means of thought processes. In both the natural sciences and the humanities, deductive thinking plays an important role in the acquisition of new knowledge and insights.

This principle should also be applied when reading the Bible. Many of God's thoughts would remain a closed book if deductive logic were not employed. If all implied conclusions had to be expounded in the Bible, it would have had to consist of many volumes. But God has given us only this one Book and also the gift of logical thought, so that we can deduce many things for ourselves. Three important examples follow:

1 Wives for Adam's sons: The frequently asked question about wives for Adam's sons is not answered explicitly in the Bible. But it is not necessary, since the answer can easily be inferred. We read in Genesis 5:4: "Adam lived 800 years and had other sons and daughters." He could have had a very large number of children! The only marriages possible were those between brothers and sisters, as well as their offspring. It would take many centuries after the Fall for the genetic copying mistakes (mutations) to build up to a level which would make close intermarriage biologically harmful. Abraham was still able to marry his half-sister; marriages between close relatives were only prohibited by God centuries later, at the time of Moses (Leviticus 18).

In the next example Jesus teaches us something about deductive (or inferential) thinking:

2 God is not a God of the dead: When He called Moses, God said: "I am the God of your father, the God of Abraham, the God of Isaac and the God of Jacob" (Exodus 3:6). The way Jesus uses these words inferentially, as a basis for the doctrine of the resurrection of the dead, is quite astounding. We read in Matthew 22:31-33: "But about the resurrection of the dead – have you not read what God said to you (Ex 3:6), 'I am the God of Abraham, the God of Isaac, and the God of Jacob?' He is not the God of the dead but of the living. When the crowds heard this, they were astonished at his teaching." Since God is life, He can only be God of the living. But Abraham, Isaac and Jacob have died, so He can only be their God if they still exist.

Here is a third example of deductive thought:

3 Concluding from creation that there is a Creator: Romans 1:19-20 especially exhorts us to apply our deductive abilities. The reasoning is as follows: By observing the objects and life forms in the universe around us, we can conclude that there must be a Creator: "What may be known about God, is plain to them, because God has made it plain to them. For since the creation of the world God's invisible qualities – his eternal power and divine nature – have been clearly seen, being understood from what has been made, so that men are without any excuse."

This illustrated book relies on the created gift of deductive thought. Not by way of proof, but by contemplation and consideration of God's works, one may discover for oneself that there must be a Creator. To avoid this conclusion, one needs to undertake substantial intellectual contortions.

Like God, we can write

The Bible mentions only two occasions when God wrote something. The first time was on Mount Sinai when He gave Moses the Ten Commandments: "When the Lord finished speaking to Moses on Mount Sinai, he gave him the two tablets of the Testimony, the tablets of stone inscribed by the finger of God" (Ex 31:18). The second time was at the feast of king Belshazzar: "Suddenly the fingers of a human hand appeared and wrote on the plaster of the wall, near the lampstand in the royal palace. The king watched the hand as it wrote. His face turned pale and he was so frightened that his knees knocked together and his legs gave way" (Dan 5:5-6). "Therefore he sent the hand that wrote the inscription. This is the inscription that was written: MENE, MENE,

TEKEL, PARSIN. This is what these words mean: God has numbered the days of your reign and brought it to an end. You have been weighed on the scales and found wanting. Your kingdom is divided and given to the Medes and Persians" (Dan 5:24-28).

The Bible mentions only one case of Jesus writing, when an adulterous woman was brought to Him: "But Jesus bent down and started to write on the ground with his finger" (John 8:6, 8). God and Jesus both wrote with their fingers!

Various writing systems have been devised by man, who is now able to record thoughts and ideas. The invention of writing is one of the greatest achievements of the human intellect. The human memory span is brief and the storage capacity of the brain, though vast, is limited. Both these problems are overcome by recording information in writing. Written information can communicate over vast distances; written records may last for many years, even centuries. Only nations possessing the skill of writing can develop literature, historiography, and high levels of technology. Nations and tribes without writing are thus restricted to a certain level of cultural development. Written language offers the possibility of storing information so that inventions and discoveries (like medical and technological advances) are not lost, but can be developed even further.

Like God, we are creative

God created everything, and the results of His creative acts exhibit such advanced concepts that we stand amazed. Here also, His thoughts, as expressed in the works of creation, are very much higher than ours. One only has to consider the ingenious information storage system in DNA molecules, or the incomprehensible wonders of the brain.

Like God, we are also able to create and to invent, although at a distinctly different level. Man's creativeness – a gift of God – is obvious when one considers writing and literature, various techno-

logical achievements (like automobiles, computers, and moon rockets), as well as the multitudes of new ideas and solutions to problems.

Like God, we can appreciate and create beautiful things

In the Sermon on the Mount Jesus points out an important characteristic of his creation: "See how the lilies of the field grow. They do not labor or spin. Yet I tell you that not even Solomon in all his splendour was dressed like one of these" (Matthew 6:28-29). God made his creation aesthetically very pleasing. Just consider the rich colourfulness of blossoms, butterflies, beetles, birds, barracuda and other fishes, or the variety of forms displayed by snowflakes, flowers, or leaves.Our ability to appreciate form and beauty is also a gift of God, as is artistic talent. Some of us can create music, literature or paintings, while others can appreciate and enjoy these works of art. Our clothes, homes and gardens are not only chosen on practical grounds, but also for aesthetic reasons.

Like God, we have our own will

God's will is mentioned very frequently in the Bible, the first time being "Let us make man." This emphasises His will in creation. Our salvation is also grounded in God's will: God "wants all men to be saved and to come to a knowledge of the truth" (1 Tim 2:4). Something of God's free will is apparent in Romans 9:18, 21: "God has mercy on whom he wants to have mercy, and he hardens whom he wants to harden ... Does not the potter have the right to make out of the same lump of clay some pottery for noble purposes and some for common use?" Another important passage in this regard is 1 Corinthians 1:26-29: "Brothers, think of what you were when you were called. Not many of you were wise by human standards; not many were influential; not many were of noble birth. But God chose the foolish things of the world to shame the wise; God chose the weak things of the world to shame the strong. He chose the lowly things of the world and the despised things – and the things that are not – to nullify the things that are, so that no one may boast before him." It becomes clear that God's will is involved, whenever one comes to faith. The way this happens, and to what extent, remains for us an unfathomable mystery. But it is nonetheless certain that, just as God has a free will, we also have been given a free will:

- God did not create puppets which can only do what the puppeteer wants.
- He did not create robots which function according to pre-determined programs.
- He did not create trained creatures, mindlessly carrying out their practised routines – we are not performing circus animals.

We have to keep in mind that our will has also been adversely affected in this fallen world. Even the great apostle Paul confesses: "For what I do is not the good I want to do; no, the evil I do not want to do – this I keep on doing" (Rom 7:19).

We have been given great freedom, with the result that:

- We can choose between heaven and hell. A greater range of choice can scarcely be imagined.
- We can wage wars, but also live in peace.
- We can do good or evil. This covers a very wide area – from the horrors of Auschwitz to the sacrificial services of many a missionary.

God observes everything with great patience, but He will eventually and definitely judge everybody: "The dead were judged according to what they had done as recorded in the books" (Rev 20:12).

Like God, we can evaluate and judge

God evaluates our lives in judgment: "we will all stand before God's judgment seat" (Rom 14:10). And we read in 2 Corinthians 5:10: "For we must all appear before the judgment seat of Christ, that each one may receive what is due him for the things done while in the body, whether good or bad." We too are able to analyse our life and situations, to set priorities, and to evaluate completed tasks and solutions. But we should not judge and condemn one another: "So then, each of us will give an account of himself to God. Therefore let us stop passing judgment on one another. Instead, make up your mind not to put any stumbling-block or obstacle in your brother's way" (Rom 14:12-13).

Like God, we can love

"God is love", as we read in 1 John 4:16. If we belong to God, we will also radiate love: "All men will know that you are my disciples, if you love one another" (John 13:35), and all Christians should be recognised by their love: "Do everything in love" (1 Cor 16:14). The well-known British evangelist Charles H. Spurgeon (1834 – 1892) put it this way: "As long as you live, do everything for the love of Christ. Let your hands and fingers work love, let your brain and eyes radiate love, fight in love, pray with love, speak lovingly, and live a life of love."

Love, compassion and mercy are related. Here also God is the First Cause: "Praise be to the God and Father of our Lord Jesus Christ, the Father of compassion" (2 Cor 1:3). Consequently, we should also practise this ability: "Be merciful, just as your Father is merciful" (Luke 6:36).

Like God, we can be faithful and true

Another characteristic of God is faithfulness: "If we are faithless, he will remain faithful, for he cannot disown himself" (2 Tim 2:13). His faithfulness never falters. What God has promised, He will carry out. During Old Testament times God continually promised that the Saviour would come. This promise was fulfilled when Jesus came at the most appropriate moment: "But when the time had fully come, God sent his Son" (Gal 4:4). God also made several covenants with people, like that with Noah (Gen 8:21 – 9:17), with Abraham (Gen 15:7-21, 17:3-14), and on Mount Sinai (Ex 19 – 24). There never was a better covenantal partner than God Himself.

Faithfulness implies an inner attitude which keeps us to our promises and duties. This fundamental trustworthiness is closely connected with truth and righteousness. The phrase "in good faith" refers to an oral treaty which is regarded as being just as binding as a written one. All human faithfulness is based on and derives from God's good faith. Marriage as an institution of God is founded on faithfulness. He expects us to be true in our daily life and also to Him: "Be faithful, even to the point of death, and I will give you the crown of life" (Rev 2:10).

We are able to commune with God, just as He communes with us

To have communion with somebody, means to have a very close mutual relationship of give and take. According to Colossians 1:16 we have been created by and for Christ. This was the purpose of creation and we have been made to have communion with our Creator. But this relationship was destroyed by man's fall into sin, like a broken marriage. In both cases the partners have lost their original close communion, resulting in tears and heartache.

Only by way of a thoroughgoing repentance and conversion to Christ (see following chapter) can communion with God and his Son be restored. In the New Testament a short formula is used to describe this restored relationship with our Creator, namely being "in Christ". This phrase is used 80 times, for example in 2 Corinthians 5:17: "if anyone is in Christ, he is a new creation." This new relationship is close and intimate, as described by Paul in Galatians 2:20: "I no longer live, but Christ lives in me". The purpose of creation has been restored. Whoever belongs to Christ will also want to regularly fellowship with other Christians.

Paul describes believers, with their various natural and spiritual talents, as being members of one body, and all together they are members of the body of Christ (1 Cor 12:27). When partaking of the Lord's Supper, we celebrate our communion with Christ. The apostle John describes the restored communion in the following words: "so that you also may have fellowship with us. And our fellowship is with the Father and with his Son, Jesus Christ" (1 John 1:3).

The consequences of communion with Christ are far-reaching:

– we share Christ's life (Rom 6:8)
– we share His resurrection (Col 2:12)
– we are co-heirs with Christ (Rom 8:17)
– we will be raised in His glory (Rom 8:17)
– we will reign with Him (2 Tim 2:12).

Further human characteristics which distinguish us from the animals

The above ten aspects are only true for human beings, and clearly separate us from the animals. We want to emphasise this here, since we are continually bombarded, in many ways, with the idea that we have descended from some line of animals. A few further aspects of being human are:

– We are historical beings. We record past events, retell them, contemplate them, and sometimes we even learn from them.

– We yearn to know a cause for things, to have an explanatory world and life view for all of reality. Only human beings are concerned with their origin, with the purpose of life, and with where we are going.

– Only human beings contemplate death and bury our dead. Eternity has been put in our hearts (Eccl 3:11). One look at the pyramids of Gizeh establishes this fact. The Egyptians knew of life after death, and they tried to provide for it according to their ideas.

Does God also have sense organs?

We read the following words of Jesus in John 4:24: "God is spirit, and his worshippers must worship in spirit and in truth." And in the first commandment God prohibits the making of physical structures supposed to represent Him:

"I am the LORD your God ... You shall not make for yourself an idol in the form of anything in heaven above or on the earth beneath or in the waters below" (Ex 20:2, 4).

Nevertheless, the Bible frequently refers to God's sense organs, and also to His mouth, His hand, His arm, His finger, and His heart:

Ear: God can hear. The Psalmist experienced this positively: "Because he (God) turned his ear to me, I will call on him as long as I live" (Ps 116:2). King Hezekiah prayed that God would listen and look: "Give ear, O LORD, and hear; open your eyes, O LORD, and see" (2 Kings 19:16). God heard the cries of the oppressed nation (Ex 3:7), their tears and groans (Psalm 6:9; Ps 102:20), their grumbling (Ex 16:7, Numbers 12:2), but also their prayers and pleas (1 Kings 8:28; 1 Kings 9:3). These can be summarised in the words of the Psalmist: "Does he who implanted the ear, not hear?" (Ps 94:9).

Eye: God's eyes miss nothing: "For the eyes of the LORD range throughout the earth to strengthen those whose hearts are fully committed to him" (2 Chron 16:9). God even sees everything that is concealed from us: "your eyes saw my unformed body" (Ps 139:16). He perceives the future and everything else which is invisible for us. Nobody can hide himself from God's eyes (Ps 139:3, 7).

Mouth: God does have a mouth, since in the creation account the words "And God said" appear ten times. Everything coming from God's mouth, is, by definition, His Word. We cannot live apart from His Word: "man does not live on bread alone but on every word that comes from the mouth of the LORD" (Deut 8:3). God gave us a mouth as well: "Who gave man his mouth? ... Is it not I, the LORD?" (Ex 4:11).

Hand: God says: "See, I have engraved you on the palms of my hands" (Is 49:16). Not only are the names of those who believe in God written in the book of life, but they are entrusted to His hand as well. Jesus "was pierced for our transgressions, he was crushed for our iniquities" (Is 53:5). His hands and feet were pierced because of our sins. The above mentioned text (Is 49:16) can thus be interpreted as: "We are engraved in the hands of Jesus". God cares for us, but also for all creatures. According to Psalm 145:16 everything is a gift from God's hand: "You open your hand and satisfy the desires of every living thing." God's hand is also involved in his works of creation, as mentioned frequently:

Psalm 19:1: "...the skies proclaim the works of his hands."
Psalm 102:25: "the heavens are the work of your hands."
Psalm 8:6: "You made him ruler over the works of your hands."

When the "good news about the Lord Jesus" (Acts 11:20) was told in Antioch, many people believed, because "The Lord's hand was with them (the apostles), and a great number of people believed and turned to the Lord" (Acts 11:21).

Arm: God's arm symbolises His great power. He led the Israelites out of Egypt with His strong arm (Acts 13:17: "with an high arm brought he them out", King James Version). God reminds doubters of His unlimited power: "Was my arm too short to ransom you? Do I lack the strength to rescue you?" (Is 50:2). God's arm is also mentioned in regard to creation: "With my great power and outstretched arm I made the earth and its people and the animals that are on it" (Jer 27:5).

Finger: God wrote the Ten Commandments with His finger (Ex 31:18). But the entire universe is also the work of His fingers: "When I consider your heavens, the work of your fingers, the moon and the stars, which you have set in place" (Ps 8:3).

Heart: There are people who are especially close to our heart; similarly, when something moves us deeply, we are touched to the heart. This is also said of God. The phrase "He has watched over your journey through this vast desert" (Deut 2:7) is rendered in the German translation as "zu Herzen genommen" – He has taken their journey "to His heart". David found favour in the eyes of God, and He testified about him: "I have found David son of Jesse a man *after my own heart*; he will do everything I want him to do" (Acts 13:22).

Every person – known to God?

Job said about his servants: "Did not he who made me in the womb, make them? Did not the same one form us both within our mothers?" (Job 31:15). God knew Jeremiah even before his conception: "Before I formed you in the womb, I knew you, before you were born, I set you apart; I appointed you as a prophet to the nations" (Jer 1:5). Isaiah also asserts: "Listen to me, you islands; hear this you distant nations: Before I was born, the LORD called me; from my birth he has made mention of my name" (Is 49:1).

As early as the embryonic stage God already knows our life history: "For you created my inmost being; you knit me together in my mother's womb. I praise you because I am fearfully and wonderfully made; your works are wonderful, I know that full well. My frame was not hidden from you when I was made in the secret place. When I was woven together in the depths of the earth, your eyes saw my unformed body. All the days ordained for me were written in your book before one of them came to be" (Ps 139:13-16).

Paul asserts that God set him apart from birth, and called him by His grace (Gal 1:15). Even still-born babies and miscarriages are mentioned in the Bible:

"A man may have a hundred children and live many years; yet no matter how long he lives, if he cannot enjoy his prosperity and does not receive proper burial, I say that a stillborn child is better off than he. It comes without meaning, it departs in darkness, and in darkness its name is shrouded. Though it never saw the sun or knew anything, it has more rest than does that man" (Eccl 6:3-5).

We should realise that God already knows our life history from the moment of conception when we are microscopically small, an unformed zygote. My career, my place in life, my vocation – God knows everything beforehand. This does not mean that our destiny is fixed so that we cannot do anything else. No, the Bible does not acknowledge such fatalism, since "It is for freedom that Christ has set us free" (Gal 5:1). The prodigal son had the freedom to leave his father's house, but after he had come to his senses, he had the freedom to return. In his omniscience God knows beforehand what we will decide.

Man after the fal

The attributes of God shared by man when he was created were to a great extent marred by sin. The Bible frequently emphasises the drastic changes involved:

Romans 3:22b-23: "There is no difference, for all have sinned and fall short of the glory of God."

Jeremiah 16:4: "They will die of deadly diseases. They will not be mourned or buried, but will be like refuse lying on the ground... their dead bodies will become food for the birds of the air and the beasts of the earth."

Psalm 144:4: "Man is like a breath; his days are like a fleeting shadow."

Ecclesiastes 3:19: "Man's fate is like that of the animals; the same fate awaits them both: As one dies, so dies the other."

Romans 1:21: "their foolish hearts were darkened."

Ephesians 4:18: "They are darkened in their understanding and separated from the life of God."

Being far from God, human thought is subject to all possible fallacies and confusions. This is very obviously the case for evolutionary ideas, ideologies, manmade religions, and all possible atheistic systems. Thus we find many scholars giving decidedly negative evaluations of humanity:

Friedrich von Schlegel (1772 – 1829), who was a German cultural philosopher and linguist: Man is ultimately no different from any animal, plant or rock.

The German nihilistic philosopher, Friedrich Nietzsche (1844 – 1900): Man is a brute as well as a super-animal. He is merely a "cosmic fringe-dweller".

The American geneticist of Russian extraction, Theodosius Dobzhansky (1900 – 1975): Man is the only product of evolution that has attained the insight that he came into this universe, from the animal kingdom, through evolution.

Jaques Monod (1910 - 1976), a French biochemist and Nobel laureate: Man is a gipsy at the edge of the universe.

The atheist Theo Löbsack: Man is only an "evolutionary aberration".

Ludwig E. Boltzmann (1844 – 1905), who was professor of theoretical physics at the University of Vienna, was completely committed to Darwinism. He regarded the idea (that life originated without a Creator), as the grandest concept of the century: "In my opinion Darwin's theory promises only the best for philosophy. If you ask me whether this time (the 19th century) should be called the iron age or the steam age or the age of electricity, I would immediately reply that it should be known as the age of a mechanistic view of nature – it will be known as the age of Darwin."

Today steadily increasing numbers of scientists regard the theory of evolution as the greatest fallacy of the century. (This topic is discussed more fully in two other books of the present author, namely: *In the Beginning was Information* and *Did God Use Evolution?* We will thus not pursue it further here). However, the following example illustrates the compulsion exerted by

- a distorted image

evolutionary thought. It concerns the difficulties of human birth. Josef H. Reichholf discusses this in an article "Difficult birth for humans – easy in the case of animals" (in the German magazine *Natur*, July 1989, p 57 - 59). He describes the birth process in the case of some mammals under the heading "Privilege of the animals: Birth without pain".

1 Giraffe: "The newborn calf falls from a height of more than two metres. But the entire birth proceeds with very little drama, in relaxed and tranquil fashion."

2 Gnu: "The heavily pregnant cow moves along with the herd, only drawing apart just before giving birth to a large, well-developed calf, without haste or complaint. She licks the calf dry, massages him, and helps the gangly newborn gnu onto his feet as necessary. From then on, he can manage on his own. The actual birth takes only a few minutes, but even this can be too long should danger threaten. Then the cow simply interrupts the birth process and runs along, with the calf already protruding, until it can emerge in safety."

3 Seals: "On the other side of the earth, the normally slender female seals, their bodies now distended, waddle clumsily over the lava rocks onto the beaches of the Galápagos islands. There, during the weeks before Christmas, they await the birth of their pups. Seals also give birth rapidly, which might be expected in view of the ease with which the streamlined body of the newborn overcomes the narrowness of the birth canal. The process is smooth and precise; only a matter of a few seconds, involving neither pain nor difficulty."

After considering other animals as well, Reichholf concludes: "Wherever we observe the birth of mammals, it seems to be relatively effortless and appropriate to their way of life." Then he comes to human beings:

"Only man doesn't fit this pattern. Usually only one baby is born, and it involves a lot of pain. And worse still – without assistance, the mother-to-be is practically helpless, especially if it is her first child." Then Reichholf again asks the question as to the "why" of the difficulty of human birth. He answers as follows:

"Why is it so hard for humans, of all creatures, to come into the world? This end-product of evolution regards itself as the crown of creation. Yet one has the impression that something must have gone wrong, something important, during man's descent. This is the logical conclusion from comparison to the other higher mammals."

Reichholf's observations are perfectly correct, but his conclusion is erroneous. Nature never explains itself. We thus require an external source of information. And the moral of the above is: Without the Bible, we are left to grope in the dark as far as most aspects of life are concerned. No biologist or gynaecologist can really explain why human childbirth is so difficult and painful. It is a direct consequence of man's sin. In the original creation painless birth was provided. But after they had sinned, God told Eve: "I will greatly increase your pains in childbearing; with pain you will give birth to children" (Gen 3:16).

The real damage caused by the theory of evolution is not so much that, seen through those glasses, many facts concerning life and nature cannot be explained satisfactorily. The real harm is that it is associated with a rejection or distortion of the Bible. Paul's assertion that he believes everything that is written (Acts 24:14), is also very important for us, as will become clear in subsequent chapters where the question of our salvation is discussed.

A very special man: Jesus

Today many people ask - who is Jesus?

Sixty thousand biographies have been written about Jesus Christ. No other historical person has been portrayed as frequently as He. Napoleon Bonaparte (1769 – 1821) said that people will for ever speak of Jesus, and many will die for Him. "But well after I am gone, nobody will speak of me (Napoleon), nor would they die for me anymore."

Nobody had to die for Jesus; He has never asked that of anybody. But it is true that, nevertheless, thousands and even millions of people willingly sacrificed their lives for Him. They only had to utter one word of retraction to be set free. But they remained faithful and accepted death rather than to disavow Him. They did this because they loved Him; never were they coerced.

Napoleon's soldiers were forced to die for him, but today nobody would even consider dying for Napoleon. The historian Kenneth Scott Latourette came to the conclusion:

"As the centuries pass the evidence is accumulating that, measured by His effect of history, Jesus is the most influential life ever lived on this planet. That influence appears to be mounting." (American Historical Review, LIV, January, 1949).

Is Jesus the Son of God? Consider the following verdicts:

1 God: When Jesus was baptised, a voice sounded from heaven. It was God Himself Who said: "This is my Son, whom I love; with him I am well pleased" (Matt 3:17). God refers to His Son, so He must be Jesus' Father. On the mountain of the transfiguration God repeated this assertion:

"This is my Son, whom I love. Listen to him!" (Mark 9:7).

2 Peter: He was a follower of Jesus and observed everything closely. He knew all the deeds of Jesus, all his words, his way of life, and his dealings with people. When Jesus asked this disciple who He was, Peter replied: "You are the Christ, the Son of the living God" (Matt 16:16).

3 A Roman centurion: A Roman centurion was in charge of the crucifixion of Jesus. He had travelled widely in the great Roman empire, which extended from England to North Africa, and from Spain to the Orient. He had fought in many battles, and was often in charge of crucifixions, the horrible and extremely painful Roman method of execution. Time after time it ws the same: persons nailed to a cross started to curse and scold. They accused those who brought them. It was always a scene of horror, groaning and agonised anger.

For the first time in his life he now experiences a crucifixion where everything is different. No evil words come from the Man on the cross, no reproach or accusation. On the contrary: He prays for the spectators. This is all the more astounding, since the people are still mocking and taunting Him. His response is quite different to that of any other person. He calls on God, praying: "Father, forgive them, for they do not know what they are doing" (Luke 23:34). The centurion also hears Jesus' barely comprehensible promise to the criminal who has confessed his guilt: "I tell you the truth, today you will be with me in paradise" (Luke 23:43). The centurion pays close attention to every word of this Man in the middle, and comes to the conclusion: "Surely he was the Son of God!" (Matt 27:54).

For Christians the double name Jesus Christ is the briefest declaration of faith, since it means that Jesus of Nazareth is the promised Christ (anointed one or Messiah – Hebrew *mashiyach*). Jesus' favourite title for Himself was the Son of Man. In this way He confirms but also conceals His position as Messiah (e. g. Matt 8:20, John 3:14). By choosing this title, He emphasises two aspects:

Firstly, that He was a human being, a descendant of human forebears. Both genealogies in Matthew 1:1-17 and Luke 3:23-38 confirm this.

Secondly, Jesus confirms and describes His second coming in glory in the following words: "For as the lightning comes from the east and is visible in the west, so will be the coming of the Son of Man... They will see the Son of Man coming on the clouds of the sky, with power and great glory" (Matt 24:27, 30). With these words, Jesus was identifying with the prophecy in Daniel Chapter 7 verse 13: "there before me was one like a *son of man*, coming with the clouds of heaven."

The Bible testifies that Jesus exists from eternity (Everlasting Father, Isaiah 9:6) to eternity: "Jesus Christ is the same yesterday and today and forever" (Hebr 13:8). When He was on earth, He was here both as God's Son and as a human being. This is expressed clearly in Philippians 2:6-7: "Who, being in very nature God, did not consider equality with God something to be grasped, but made himself nothing, taking the very nature of a servant, being made in human likeness."

God is calling everyone

The greatest catastrophe that ever befell humanity was not the Second World War, neither was it any of history's mass famines, nor even one of the great plague epidemics. It was man's fall into sin. Not just thousands or millions of people, but the entire human race was struck by the deadly torpedo of sin. Sin has one very malicious property. It spreads like a virulent epidemic, causing death and destruction ever since the very first transgression. All human beings are infected by this horrible disease. During the course of our life we contribute in no small way to the multiplication of sin's effects. Sin is a law unto itself, so that in our fallen nature, we cannot avoid it. Thus we read in Romans 7:19: "For what I do is not the good I want to do; no, the evil I do not want to do – this I keep on doing."

What is sin? First and foremost, sin is our separation from God. Our sinful acts are consequences of this general condition. "All wrongdoing is sin" (1 John 5:17).

The Ten Commandments, as given by God in Exodus 20:1-17, are like a mirror by which we can judge our deeds. Jesus expounds the Commandments in depth in the Sermon on the Mount (Matthew chapters 5 to 7). Not only is the actual deed sin, but also the preceding thoughts in our heart. The slightest deviation from these unchangeable standards of God is sin, and by this standard, nobody is righteous. Even when we neglect to do good, it is also sin in the eyes of God: "Anyone, then, who knows the good he ought to do and doesn't do it, sins" (Jam 4:17).

All unbelief is sin, as we read in Romans 14:23: "everything that does not come from faith is sin."

In our time occult practices like fortune-telling, pendulum swinging, and spiritism, have increased to an alarming extent. In many bookshops there are extensive collections of esoteric literature, and the souls of many readers are poisoned by these books. God warns against these abominations: "do not learn to imitate the detestable ways of the nations there. Let noone be found among you who sacrifices his son or daughter in the fire, who practises divination or sorcery, interprets omens, engages in witchcraft, or casts spells, or who is a medium or spiritist or who consults the dead. Anyone who does these things is detestable to the Lord" (Deut 18:9-12).

But the **chief sin** in the eyes of God is that people do not believe in His Son and do not follow Him. Jesus says that it is the one greatest sin if "men do not believe in me" (John 16:9). The real nature of sin and its effects becomes clear in the Greek word, *hamartia*, used in the New Testament. It means to miss the target. Through our sin we miss our life's purpose as intended by God, like an arrow which does not hit the centre of the bulls-eye. If we enter eternity with our sins, then we are lost, and will experience perdition and eternal death (Prov 14:34b, Rom 6:23a). God has said that He will not admit one single sin into His heaven: "No longer will there be any curse" (Rev 22:3). If God were to allow sin in His heaven, then even this place of glory would soon be devastated. Were sin to enter, the same fate as on earth would befall heaven: strife and fighting, enmity and jealousy, illness and suffering, distress and death. But heaven must remain heaven; a place of eternal joy and a place where everyone loves each other. How many people really love us here on earth? In most cases we can count them on the fingers of one hand. And, when asked, many people would say: "Nobody loves me; I am alone."

God Himself solved the problem of sin through Jesus: "God made him who had no sin, to be sin for us" (2 Cor 5:21). No human being can bear his own sin, because sin cannot be compensated for nor be erased by means of good deeds or religious rites. There is no medical remedy for sin, but the one Person Who could erase sin, did exactly that. We read that Jesus "himself bore our sins in his body on the tree" (= the cross on Calvary, 1 Peter 2:24). Because of this sacrifice, the possibility of salvation is there for everyone, without limit, be they:

- young or old
- rich or poor
- male or female
- illiterate or a Nobel prize-winner
- black, white, yellow, or red – God does not distinguish between races
- American, British, French, German, or Russian – with God, there are no national boundaries
- speakers of Arabic, Chinese, English, or German – God knows no language barriers

A wider range can hardly be imagined. God's plan of salvation, based on love and a free will, is not just available for 5 % or 10 % or 20 % of all human beings, but for all 100 %: Jesus "is the atoning sacrifice for our sins, and not only for ours, but also for the sins of the whole world" (1 John 2:2). The great tragedy is that only a relatively small fraction of all people find salvation by turning to Jesus (Matt 7:13-14, Luke 12:32). The rest stay on the old, wide road leading inevitably to damnation.

Two maritime parables:
the *Gustloff* and the *Titanic*

Since the discussion following concerns rescue from deadly peril, we will look at two dramatic 20th Century examples. **First**, one of the greatest shipping catastrophes of all time, the sinking of the *Gustloff* during the Second World War.

The *Wilhelm Gustloff* sailed from Gotenhafen near Danzig (now Gdansk) on Tuesday the 30th of January 1945. On board were 6,600 people, mostly refugees and wounded fleeing from East Prussia to the West. The air temperature was -18 °C as the overloaded ship plowed through a heavy sea on this icy winter night. The lookout on a half-submerged Russian submarine lying north of the town of Stolpmünde (East Pomerania) saw the outline of a large ship. At about 9:00 p. m. three torpedoes from this submarine hit the *Gustloff*. Within an hour it had sunk, costing more than 5,000 people their lives.

The ship was named after Wilhelm Gustloff, a Swiss Nazi Party functionary who had been murdered in 1936. It was used by the "German Labour Front" as their flagship for the "Strength Through Joy" movement. With a gross registered tonnage of 25,484, this luxury liner had a capacity of nearly 1,500 passengers. When war broke out, it served as a hospital and as barracks for the naval contingent stationed at Gotenhafen. As the war front moved nearer, it was one of the ships assigned to transporting refugees and soldiers towards the West. Damaged by bombs and overloaded, it could only manage 12 knots, compared to its original capability of 15.5 knots (29 km/h).

At the time there was only a low risk of enemy submarine activity, so only one destroyer escorted the ship, and a zig-zag course was deemed unnecessary. After being hit, the ship listed 15 degrees, where it stayed for about 20 minutes, then it keeled over further and further before finally sinking. Because there were nowhere near enough lifeboats, most passengers faced certain death. Only 1,252 people could be rescued from the icy waters.

The eyewitness and survivor of this catastrophe, Heinz Schön (1926 –) gives us this graphic sketch of the sinking:

"At 10:16 p. m., sixty minutes after the first torpedo hit, which was followed straight away by two more, the *Gustloff* readies herself to die. No one knows that the death struggle of this ship will last a mere two minutes more. Nobody has any idea, how many people have already had to die on the *Gustloff* in the last sixty minutes, torn apart by torpedoes, suffocated by the gases of detonation, battered to death by falling furniture, trampled to death in the stairways, drowned in the foreship, in the corridors, the chambers, the halls and in the lower promenade deck, which became a 'glass coffin'".

And then he describes the final minute:

"Now the minute of death has arrived for the *Gustloff*. For all still on board her, there will be no more rescue. They don't want to die, but death is inevitable. I also am fighting for life in the chilly Baltic Sea. Next to me hundreds of people are struggling desperately in the icy waters, clutching onto the rims of boats, with whose occupants they fight as they search for some sort of a handhold. But the relentless cold soon immobilizes their limbs. The sea tosses these hapless people around like toys. With gurgling cries for help, countless numbers have already sunk under the waves or are hanging lifeless in their bouyancy vests.

"I'm amazed to still be conscious. My eyes try to penetrate the darkness. The massive swell lifts me to towering heights, only to let me sink again into deep wave valleys. Will no rescue come? If ships don't arrive soon, then all those struggling in the water here will soon be death's prize. I wasn't to know that at this very moment, only about 100 metres from the stricken vessel, the torpedo boat *Löwe* was already taking the first of the survivors on board.

"Many sets of eyes are now staring at the sinking colossus as she readies herself for dying; now the very second of her death has arrived for the ship. A loud booming sound comes from the *Gustloff*, as the last bulkheads are broken. The ship is listing more and more, as the screaming of those still on board reaches a crescendo. As the wreck tilts even further, suddenly the unexpected happens. As if controlled by a ghostly hand, in an instant the entire ship's lighting comes on – the vessel shines in full splendour, looking like a magnificent apparition. The *Gustloff* goes down with full festive lighting. As if illuminated by the glow of her carefree days of peacetime, reflected a thousand-fold in the foaming ocean, the sinking coffin tips towards the waves and plunges into a watery grave. Blinded by the light, clusters of writhing people, bunched like grapes, spill overboard from the twenty metre wide sundeck, a scream of despair on their lips before they hit the water.

"What now - another ghostly happening? The ship's siren starts operating, all by itself, herald-ing the end of the *Gustloff*. A long drawn-out howling sound fills the air, then becomes weaker and hoarser. Then the howling siren is choked off, the light extinguished. The ship is dead – it sinks finally into the surging waters. A massive moun-tain of water crashes over the *Gustloff*, extin-guishing the very last death cry."

(Heinz Schön: *Die Gustloff-Katastrophe*, Motor-buch Verlag Stuttgart, 4. Auflage 1995 pp 332, 335-336)

Another never-to-be-forgotten tragedy of mari-time voyaging, one which is probably the best-known worldwide, occurred in the year 1912. It was the sinking of the **Titanic**. On her maiden voy-age, she was already set on a course to her death.

The trauma of this story has remained to this day. The *Titanic* was regarded as the most signifi-cant ship of 1912. Costing more than seven mil-lion dollars, she was the largest movable object ever made by human hands. She was a sky-scraper among ships, an oceanic giant four street blocks long, and eleven stories high. The shipping company, White Star Line, was exceptionally proud of her, giving this luxury liner the label "unsinkable". The bulkheads to her 16 compart-ments could be individually closed to make them watertight; even if two of these compartments

filled with water, the *Titanic* would float on. This was one of the reasons why the usual safety requirements were only partially fulfilled. For instance, there were only enough lifeboats for every second person on board.

On April 10, 1912 the *Titanic* left Southampton in the south of England on her maiden voyage, bound for New York. Among the more than 2,200 people on board were some of the richest people on earth. Also some of the poorest, wanting to make a new life in America. Both the famous and the forgotten were on the passenger list. A suite for the journey cost 5,000 dollars. Not surprising-ly, morale and atmosphere on board was excel-lent; after all, the ship was the world's fastest and safest, catering for its passengers' every pos-sible need. No one imagined that any harm could befall her. Iceberg warnings, among them those from the German ship *Amerika*, were widely ignored, since the *Titanic* was supposed to be especially invulnerable to iceberg damage.

On the night of April 14, the world's first and only "unsinkable" ship was about 400 nautical miles east of Newfoundland. Not a single cloud obscured the glittering stars on this moonless, bitterly cold night. The unusually dead calm con-ditions made the surface of the Atlantic appear like a sheet of polished glass. At 11:40 p. m. on Sunday, April the 14th, 1912, as the *Titanic* knifed through the smooth black sea, her starboard (right) side scraped along a massive iceberg, pro-truding about 30 metres above the water. A hor-rendous, 91 metre long gash opened up in the 269 metre long hull.

The *Titanic* was now a death ship, with no one yet aware of it. Most of the passengers were in their cabins. A few crew members still sat talking in the first class dining salon on D deck. As they spoke, a vague grinding sound, not particularly loud at first, came from somewhere deep within the ship. The faint jangling of cutlery, laid out for tomor-row's breakfast, provided the only other hint of any disturbance on this so-far-flawless cruise.

Passengers woken by the bump tried to somehow correlate it with familiar events. Someone said

'That's funny – we're docking!' Another thought that a heavy wave must have struck the ship. One woman, awoken by the grinding scrape, said it was 'as if a giant finger was dragged along the flank of the ship'. Mrs Astor, the wife of the richest man on board, thought there must have been a mishap in the kitchen.

Other than that, there was nothing apart from this sound, grotesque in its apparent harmlessness. Some called it a scratching, others a scraping sound, still others a dragging or even a grinding noise. Most passengers slept through and heard nothing. Some leaving the smoking lounge stepped out on deck just in time to be able to catch a glimpse of the iceberg scraping alongside. In the next instant it had disappeared into the darkness. The momentary excitement soon settled; the *Titanic* still seemed as massive and solid as ever, and it was much too cold to stay outside any longer. A card game seemed in order.

Till now, it had been a cruise of the purest pleasure – a liner on its maiden voyage, everything new and shiny. The confidence which reigned supreme aboard the mighty vessel had been most profoundly expressed by one steward to a Mrs Caldwell: "Even God couldn't sink this ship." But *Titanic's* death warrant had been signed. Captain Edward John Smith didn't hurry to the radio to announce the collision, but went first to notify the billionaire, John Jacob Astor, before anyone else. This is when Astor is supposed to have uttered the now-famous words, "I ordered ice, indeed, but this is ridiculous!"

Over the next two and a half hours, the bow sank ever deeper, until the enormous weight of the now-protruding stern caused the vessel to suddenly break in two. The now-separated bow section sank first. Shortly after, the stern rose almost horizontally out of the water, before this portion of the ship, too, plunged down towards the floor of the icy Atlantic, 3,821 metres below. Since boiler operators and machinists had been instructed to keep the machinery for power generation going as long as possible, all the *Titanic's* lights were shining brightly, some even staying on while already under water. This eerie illumination

of the silent catastrophe continued right up to just two minutes before the ship sank completely beneath the ocean surface.

1522 people lost their lives; only 712, barely a third of those on board, were rescued. The proportion of those rescued was significantly different according to their class (first class: 62%; second class: 42.5%; third class: 25.5%). Almost anything else might have seemed conceivable – the champagne running out, an epidemic breaking out among the third class passengers, perhaps even the bandmaster falling asleep. But no one would have dreamt for a minute that this proud ship would, on the night of the 14th through 15th April, 1912, after contacting an iceberg, simply sink and plunge 1500 people into an icy grave in the North Atlantic.

It was precisely 2:20 a. m. on the 15th April 1912 when the mighty vessel sank into the depths of the sea. Since that moment, the *Titanic* has become a metaphor for pride preceding a downfall.

In 1985, 73 years after the catastrophe, the wreck was located, at a depth of 3,800 metres, by Robert Ballard, underwater geologist at the Woods Hole Oceanographic Institution in Massachusetts, USA. Situated south of Newfoundland, it was strewn over an area the size of the city of London. Resting in the ocean depths, the *Titanic* is like some irresistible emotional powerhouse. Her tragic story, revisited over and over, has spawned thousands of books, and some three dozen films – including the 1997 epic by American director James Cameron.

Cameron's blockbuster film "Titanic" turned the catastrophe into a box-office bonanza. Millions of moviegoers worldwide shared the experience of being on board the most renowned passenger liner of all time during an elaborate cinematic reconstruction of her sinking. With the largest single set yet constructed, Cameron's film was the most successful in the history of the movies. The real *Titanic* cost a handsome 7.5 million dollars 85 years before – the screen version devoured 200 million dollars, making it the most expensive film of all time. It took only 26 days to recover these costs at the box office. Director Cameron said of the original catastrophe, "The *Titanic* is a drama about faith in technology, and the bankruptcy of everything she promised in the name of progress. I regard this story as a perfect characterisation of our 20th Century. We are all in a sense living on a kind of *Titanic*."

Both these big ships seemed safe and secure to their passengers, but from a particular moment on, they were set on a course of death, their doom sealed and certain. The only possibility of escaping death was via the lifeboats, of which there were insufficient for the large number of people who needed them. In both cases, there was ample time for rescue.

Both these maritime tragedies, the *Gustloff* and the *Titanic*, have significant lessons for us:

– Just hours before their doom, people imagined themselves to be in great safety.
– In the midst of deadly danger, rescue was possible. But it required making a switch, a transfer, the boarding of another vessel.

We can use these historical occurrences to draw a parallel with another catastrophe, the greatest one ever experienced by mankind, namely the Fall into sin. The torpedo strike (or iceberg gash) suffered by the ship of humanity at the Fall set it irrevocably on a path to doom, just as surely as for each of the two ships. Those who stay on board, that is, keep living just as they have been, will sink with mathematical punctuality at the tribunal of God. It is the Creator's damning verdict upon sin which brings eternal lostness in its wake: "Just as man is destined to die once, and after that to face judgment" (Hebr 9:27). Here too, only a lifeboat can help. Fortunately, there is such a lifeboat – provided by God Himself! Here, also, you need to make the required transfer, to board the vessel, in order to be saved.

Let us now apply several aspects of the accounts of the *Gustloff* and *Titanic* to the ship of humanity. This ship is carrying various groups of people: Evangelicals and Catholics, churchgoers and non-churchgoers, atheists and Buddhists, Muslims

and Hindus. The representatives of all the world's religions and all its political parties are on board, as well as followers of all manner of schools of philosophical thought. The exhortation to get on board the lifeboat applies to all of them – from wherever anyone might be. May what follows become a saving wake up call, that we might escape being eternally lost. The Bible speaks dramatically of this escape: "How shall we escape [i.e. escape hell, escape eternal damnation] if we ignore such a great salvation [i.e. God's lifeboat, Jesus Christ]?" (Hebr 2:3).

Although the passengers represent widely different systems of thought, they all have one thing in common – the ship they are on is doomed. The only way they can be saved is if salvation comes from outside. Man's salvation is thus the main theme of the Bible. Some important points in this regard:

– God has devised a plan of salvation which is available to every human being, in contrast to those on board the *Gustloff* or the *Titanic*.

– God has prepared an enormous lifeboat, known as "Jesus Christ". There is room for everyone on this lifeboat.

– There are no alternative lifeboats (John 14:6, Acts 4:12). Only this one boat is standing by.

– At the *Gustloff* sinking, dramatic scenes unfolded. Those who did manage to reach one of the overloaded lifeboats were pushed away by force, to keep the entire boat from capsizing and sinking. But nobody is ever pushed away from lifeboat Jesus!

God informs us: God has made it known to humanity that they are passengers on a ship of doom, and He Himself prepared the lifeboat. Nobody who wants to be rescued will be turned away; sufficient provision has been made for all. Those who want to be saved will eagerly board the lifeboat.

Too simple? People often object that this is far too simple. Surely salvation cannot be such a simple matter! But the mere fact that our rescue is so simple for us, demonstrates that God Himself is working. It was however very costly for Him. God said through the prophet Isaiah: "you have burdened me with your sins" (Is 43:24). In comparison, the creation of the universe was a simple task, as we read in Psalm 8:3: "When I consider your heavens, the work of your fingers." We do not have to swim three times around the floundering ship in icy waters to qualify for admission into the ark of salvation.

Not applicable: One aspect of these two parables does not apply to today's situation: At some point everybody on either ship knew that it was doomed, and they tried to leave the ship in panic. If ever in our lives we should be in a similar position, we would know exactly where we were – whether on the sinking ship or already in a lifeboat. But, in contrast, many people today are in one of two dreadful, tragic situations (T1 and T2 below):

T1: Modern man in general does not believe that he is sailing on a doomed ship. People like the music on board and are feasting at the buffet. They are not conscious of any danger and are not interested in a lifeboat.

The main purpose of this book is to convince you, dear reader, that you are in deadly danger, and to point the way to the lifeboat standing by. The process of transferring from the ship of death to the ark of salvation is known in the Bible by a special term, namely conversion! No rescue is possible from a sinking ship without boarding a lifeboat. This is also the case for eternal life, since it cannot be obtained without repentance. Jesus says in Luke 13:3: "unless you repent (change your course, leave the doomed ship by turning to Jesus), you too will all perish."

T2: There is another fatal situation on the ship of death: Some people say that they are already safe in a lifeboat, although they have not yet made the transfer. For them the danger is very great, because they see no reason for changing. In this way they might miss the lifeboat altogether and rush headlong into destruction. Who are these people?

– In the first place there are those who believe in God, but have never turned to Jesus, never been truly converted. This includes many members of mainline churches, and even pastors and elders who have never yet experienced a real breakthrough of faith. They are ensnared in traditions and customs, and know nothing of a living relationship with Jesus.

– Furthermore, there are people who actually serve Jesus, but who have also never really been converted. Recently somebody told me that he wanted to serve Jesus by studying theology, but he shied away from conversion, from a personal relationship with Jesus.

After speaking on the subject, I have repeatedly met such people who have recognised their plight from the talk, and have then repented fully.

People who belong to this group and do not respond to the call, will one day be judged by Jesus with the words He prophesied in the Sermon on the Mount: "Not everyone who says to me, 'Lord, Lord', will enter the kingdom of heav-

The Gustloff: *The* Wilhelm Gustloff *– pride of the "Strength-Through-Joy" fleet, seen from above, 1938 (Reproduced from* Die "Gustloff"-Katastrophe, *by Heinz Schön, Motorbuch Verlag, Stuttgart, p 88).*

en, but only he who does the will of my Father who is in heaven. Many will say to me on that day, 'Lord, Lord, did we not prophesy in your name, and in your name drive out devils and perform many miracles?' Then I will tell them plainly, 'I never knew you. Away from me, you evildoers!'" (Matt 7:21-23).

Isn't this remarkable? There are people who have acted in the name of Jesus, and still they are lost. We can summarise the above words of Jesus in terms of our parable: You have never left the ship of death! That is the reason why you will also perish like the unbelievers travelling on the same ship.

It is obvious that there are different groups on the ship of doom; these will now be discussed. The fate of every one of us is tied to this ship. In all, four groups of people can be distinguished (P1 to P4), and you, the reader of this book, inevitably belong to one of these groups:

P1. You are one of those who already, at some point in your life, understood your position and confessed. You have stepped over and you can say with great certainty that you have boarded the lifeboat. In this lifeboat there is a list of passengers, comprising the names of all those who boarded. The Bible calls this list the "Book of Life". Only those persons whose names appear in this book will reach the safe shore, heaven. Jesus once told such people "rejoice that your names are written in heaven" (Luke 10:20). If your name is included, I rejoice with you!

P2. Up to this point you did not know where you were, but it has now become clear to you that you are still on the doomed ship. If you leave the ship of death forthwith by accepting Jesus right now, you are rescued immediately. The simple and practical way of doing this is explained fully below in the chapter "Getting your name in the 'Book of Life'". The conversion of all persons mentioned in the New Testament always takes place at a specific time and place.

Right now, wherever you are, note the date from a calendar or your watch. Nobody ever moves

gradually from the doomed ship to the lifeboat. The actual decision and the transfer is always instantaneous, although it may be based on previous knowledge and belief. Today may become the greatest day of your life. The only requirement is that you must make a real decision and act accordingly. The example of the prodigal son illustrates this. The moment he realises his lost state, he says "*I will* set out and go back..." (Luke 15:18).

P3. You are one of those who thought they were safely in a lifeboat, but were not. Through the Holy Spirit, you have been made aware of your true situation. If you are one of these, confess your error and change today. As established earlier in T2, this group may include people who serve Jesus and consequently assume that they cannot be on the ship of death (see T2 and the Sermon on the Mount, Matthew 7:21-23). The *Gustloff* did not sink immediately, but it took 62 minutes after the torpedoes had hit. Rescue was only possible during this period. In the same way God grants us our entire life for conversion, but no one knows how long that will be. In biblical language this is known as the time of grace.

P4. You are one of those who think the ship is not in danger. So why would you climb aboard a lifeboat? I sincerely wish that none of the readers of this book belongs to this group. Why not?

People in this fourth group have even developed a scientific theory (or accepted it ready-made from others), which asserts that the doomed ship cannot go down. They have declared it to be unsinkable. This was also said of the *Titanic* which sank on its maiden voyage. The following two examples may clarify the issue:

– Recently after a lecture a student told me that there was no hell. When I asked him how he knew this, he replied that that was what his pastor taught. In other words, the doomed ship can't sink. What a tragic fallacy!

– When Jesus cried out on the cross: "It is finished" (John 19:30), it meant that the lifeboat was ready. The requirements for the salvation of everybody had now been met. I recently attended a lecture by a professor of theology, who stated that Jesus never uttered those words on the cross. What he was ultimately saying was that the completion and existence of the lifeboat was being scientifically/theologically ignored.

Those in group P4 will receive the wages of living a lie: "If anyone's name was not found written in the book of life, he was thrown into the lake of fire" (Rev 20:15).

The chapter about the book of life has been especially written for people in groups P2 and P3. Please read this section as a special personal message to you.

The *Gustloff* and the *Titanic*: further details

The ship *Wilhelm Gustloff*: The keel of "Ship No 511" was laid in August 1935, and it was

The sinking of the Gustloff: *Hit by three torpedoes, the* Wilhelm Gustloff *sinks while listing badly to port. Those of the 6,600 passengers and crew who are still alive now begin a life-and-death struggle for survival. (Drawing by H. Rathe, based on information given by eye witnesses and by Heinz Schön, one of the survivors; reproduced from his book* Ostsee '45 – Menschen, Schiffe, Schicksale *[The Baltic Sea 1945 – People, ships, and their fates], Motorbuch Verlag, Stuttgart, p 220).*

launched on the fifth of May 1937 in the shipyard of Blohm & Voss in Hamburg, in the presence of Adolf Hitler. Its length was 208.5 m, its beam measured 23.5 m, and its gross registered tonnage was 25,484. It was powered by four eight-cylinder two-stroke diesel engines driving twin propellers. During the 17 months from its maiden voyage until August 1939, it undertook 44 voyages carrying a total of 65,000 tourists. After the catastrophe of 30 January 1945 only one fifth of the passengers (1,252 persons) were rescued; in all, 5,348 people perished.

The man Wilhelm Gustloff: He was born on the 30th of January 1895 in Schwerin near Hamburg, exactly 50 years, to the day, before the ship sank. The Nazis seized power in Germany on the 30th of January 1933, and exactly 12 years later the ship came to grief. Gustloff joined the Nazi Party in 1929, and he became the national group leader for Switzerland in 1932. On the 4th of February 1936 he was fatally wounded in his house in Davos, shot by a 27 year old Jewish medical student. This student, David Frankfurter, arrived in Davos on the 30th of January 1936. Interestingly, the same date turns up four times.

On February the 12th Wilhelm Gustloff was buried with great fanfare as ordered by Göbbels, the Minister of Propaganda. There were 35,000 mourners in Schwerin, including many VIPs of the Third Reich. In his funeral oration Hitler said that Gustloff's death would be an eternal legacy for future generations of the German nation. He had thus decided to name this, the first working ship commissioned by the Nazi Party, the *Wilhelm Gustloff*. This ship is a reminder of one of the darkest chapters of German history.

The ship *Titanic*: Some figures: 46,328 gross registered tonnage, displacement at a waterline of 10.51m: 66,000 tonnes, overall length: 268.68 metres, width: 28.19 metres, height: 18.44 metres from the water surface to the boat deck, or 53.33 metres from the keel to the tip of the four massive smokestacks, drive: 3 propellers; the middle one was driven by a turbine. This propeller weighed 22 tonnes, with a diameter of 5 metres. The outer two propellers were driven by piston engines and at 7.16 metres diameter, weighed 38 tonnes. The ship's engines produced a staggering 36,800 kW of power. It could store 6,000 tonnes of coal. Its daily consumption of coal was between 620 and 640 tonnes, that is 7.3 kg each second! At full steam the *Titanic* could travel at 24-25 knots (44.5 to 46.3 km per hour).

Personal testimonies:
Jesus found through a book

Many readers may now be asking: "How can I repent? How can I disembark from the ship of death? That's what I really want to do! Could I use this book to help me do that?" The basic answer given by the Bible is that you must first hear the message of Jesus' redemption: "faith comes from hearing the message, and the message is heard through the word of Christ" (Rom 10:17). First of all the message of Jesus must come to us. This could happen through listening to an evangelistic sermon followed by pastoral counselling, by talking with an experienced Christian, or even by reading an evangelistically oriented book.

That is precisely the purpose of this book – to show you, in detail, the way of turning to Christ. The necessity of salvation was dealt with in the previous chapter. The process of redemption is explained in detail in the next chapter. But first I want to let a few people tell about their own conversions. The first testimony is of a man who came to faith in an unusual way by reading a New Testament obtained from the Gideons (an international association which distributes Bibles in many countries of the world).

From Auschwitz to Christ

From 1942 to 1944, a certain man had to operate the cremation ovens at Auschwitz. A Polish Jew, he spent nearly six years in the concentration camp. Though he hated Germans intensely, he had of necessity learnt their language.

Eventually he emigrated to Israel, broken in spirit and incapable of doing any work. After a long time he got a job at the tunnel of Hezekiah. This tunnel was commissioned by King Hezekiah, to channel water under the city of Jerusalem from the Gihon spring to the pool of Siloam. At this pool, Jesus healed the man who was born blind (John 9:7).

And it was here that this Jew found a trilingual New Testament (German, English and French) of the Gideons, left behind by a tourist. He wanted to throw it away, since he could only read the German portion, and did not want to be reminded of this hated language. He said later that he was inexplicably prevented from throwing it away. He found that he could not discard it, and he read it secretly while waiting for new groups of tourists. Eventually he had worked through the entire text, from cover to cover. He had never before heard of this Jesus Christ, but after reading just the Gospel of Matthew, which he calls the gospel for the Jews, he realised that Jesus is the long-awaited Messiah of the Jews.

For several years this New Testament provided his only spiritual nourishment. He did not know any Christian, until the day that he met a German youth who asked him to forgive the Germans for all the wrong done to the Jews. This opened his heart and for the first time he testified that he, too, believed in Jesus Christ. He then joyfully showed the youth his well-read Gideon New Testament, saying: "I believe in this Jesus. What we read here, is the truth. This Jesus is my Lord."

Further examples: After lectures in many different places I often meet people who tell me they came to faith through some special book. The following are brief testimonies from some of these, from various backgrounds, of how they were converted. I would emphasise that these three examples were chosen subjectively. They are not meant to represent any "standard" way to come to Christ, which as already mentioned could either be through a sermon, or a conversation with a Christian, or a book, for example. Their sole purpose is to help you with the step now in front of you. Such a decision must be deliberate, and in most cases it involves an inner struggle. I therefore trust that the following personal testimonies might help you.

A book that caused a restless night

I found faith in Jesus Christ at five o'clock in the morning of the 3rd October 1992. My name is Anja Raum, I am 36 years old and am now the mother of three children. My life was strongly affected by various circumstances – our first baby, giving up my career as a teacher, moving to strange surroundings, and the affliction of our daughter with neurodermatitis. I questioned the meaning of life, and wondered where my own life was headed. At that time I was speaking on the phone with my friend Jutta, who I knew was a Christian. During the conversation I asked her why the Christian faith was the only real truth, and what about all the other religions. Are they all false? Jutta sent me a copy of the book *What About the Other Religions?*. I immediately started to read it. That first night the difference between the Christian faith and the other religions already became clear, when I read the illustrative comparison, of God being on the summit of a mountain. In all the other religions people try to come closer to God by their own efforts, by means of good works, and by performing traditionally prescribed rites. It is only in the Christian faith that God comes down to man, in the person of Jesus Christ, and restores communion with Him when one accepts, by faith, Jesus' redemption and forgiveness.

The next evening I read further, and for the first time I understood what the consequences would be if I rejected this gift. It would mean that I stand guilty before God's judgment, that a second death will follow the first, involving eternal separation from God. This really struck me, unsettling me deeply. I went to bed with this unease, intending to sleep over it; at the same time I longed to be secure in God. At 5 o'clock in the morning I made my decision. For the first time in my life I really prayed in earnest – only a few sentences. I prayed that Jesus would take my life in His hands, and told Him that He died on the cross for me also. Since then I live in the joy and certainty that Jesus is the Truth. His Word, the Bible, has become very important for me, as has fellowship with other believers who have likewise experienced conversion. I was baptised on the 20th of March 1994, on the confession of my faith. Before my conversion I would never have thought that I would eventually become a mother of three children. I had been very afraid of being dependent on a man. I was also afraid of the closeness and exclusivity of nuclear family ties. Now God has blessed me with a family including three children, and, above all, with

trust and confidence about our future. My life now has a purpose and a wonderful goal, to live for God, and to learn to love Him more and more. Anja Raum (Rödermark, Germany, aged 36)

Through babywear to faith

In my search for God and the meaning of life, I didn't find answers in the church, and I didn't understand what such formal religious beliefs had to do with me. Consequently, I turned to eastern beliefs and to esoteric teachings, such as astrology, spiritualism and the like. At the height of my esoteric blindness, my husband was transferred to a remote rural town near the Dutch border, and I found myself completely isolated. We had very little contact with others, and my false esoteric beliefs caused me much anxiety and confusion. During that time of distress I was looking for clothing for my baby and I was browsing through a mail-order catalogue of a firm specialising in natural products. Quite unexpectedly for such a catalogue, I read a piece written by the lady who owned the firm. She described her personal relationship with Jesus Christ and the inner peace and happiness she had thereby obtained. I was deeply impressed by her testimony, and longed for the same peace for myself. A few books were also listed in the catalogue, and, amongst other things, I ordered a Bible, the book *Questions I have always wanted to ask*, and a book about Christian child-rearing.

I subsequently obtained a book catalogue, and for the first time I learned about books which unambiguously and clearly expounded the Christian position against esoteric/occult teaching like astrology, soothsaying, and so on. Because all my previous involvement with esoteric matters had only ever dragged me down, I was happy to find out that God regards these things as abominations and unequivocally forbids them. I subsequently destroyed all occult books and objects and broke off all contact with those people. I obtained a clear Christ-centred orientation by reading the books I had ordered. The book *Questions I have always wanted to ask* was very helpful, because it clarified many questions which troubled me, seeing that I had no Christian friends whom I could consult. The book served as a substitute friend. What was even more important: It showed me in a very practical and step-by-step way how to pray and how to entrust one's life to Jesus Christ. I followed these instructions carefully. It was very important for me to see from this book that all my steps were based on the Word of God and did not depend on my own feelings. It also dealt beforehand with doubts that might eventually have arisen. On a certain definite and unforgettable day in September 1994 Jesus Christ became my Lord and Saviour.

Ever since Jesus has become my Lord, I have been free from all the negative influences which plagued me when I had dabbled in the occult. I have experienced the living Jesus Who helps us today the moment we are prepared to entrust ourselves entirely to His hands. The time we spent in that remote town (which we have meanwhile left), now seems to me like an exile given to me to come to my senses and to find God. I am grateful and happy that God arranged things in such a way that I acquired all the books which helped me to find salvation, and provided practical guidance about praying to Jesus Christ and accepting Him as Lord and Saviour, which I found in the book *Questions I have always wanted to ask.* Astrid K. (Münster, Germany, aged 35)

Questions looking for answers

My wife Carola, and I, Lutz Meyer, accepted the Christian faith about five years ago. We are very grateful to God that we jointly came to saving faith, and I would like to briefly describe this:

I had no contact with the Christian faith for many years after participating in children's hours and in the activities of Christian youth organisations in my young days. Even when I was confirmed at a later stage, it was purely a formality, done because everybody else did it. But it did not in any way affect my relationship to God. This godless condition lasted until I was 27 years old. At that time I was already acquainted with my present wife. She experienced strong rejection during her teacher training course because of her conservative moral attitude – lecturers and fellow students simply assumed, incorrectly, that her stance reflected her Christian beliefs. God used this situation to make us question things. We looked for reasons for the emphatic rejection of, on the one hand, marriage, conjugal fidelity, family, the traditional roles of husband and wife, and, on the other hand, the intense rejection of Christianity. Because we were considering a future together as marriage partners, based on classical family roles, we grew curious. Was there a possible connection between our perception of the roles of husband and wife and the Christian faith? The aggressive approach taken by others prompted us to deeply question such things. We actually got into some rather hard discussions among ourselves, but without having any real basis to go on.

At that time we became acquainted with a refugee family through a practical assignment of my wife. Through these people, we came to understand the connection between our ideas about family, and the Christian faith. We are very grateful to God for the witness and prayers of this family, which were a great help on our way to finding faith. God used this circumstance to involve us more and more with Christianity for just over a year.

As a mechanical engineer I was interested in science, and I wanted to resolve for myself the question of "creation versus evolution". If I was going to believe the Bible, and finally have solid ground beneath my feet, I needed to believe it from beginning to end. I was not interested in philosophies and religious theories anymore; these only produced partial answers. Books like *Did God Use Evolution?* and *What About the Other Religions?* were a great help at that time.

After God had made it abundantly clear to us in various ways that we needed to be converted, certain questions still blocked the way, probably because of ignorance. Questions like: Have we really come far enough? Do we know enough? Have we changed sufficiently? Here we were greatly helped by the book *What About the Other Religions?* It showed clearly that our conversion did not depend on any prerequisites on our side.

We read the sections on repentance and rebirth once more; together we confessed our guilt before God and received forgiveness and eternal life, being for ever grateful for God's provision on Calvary. It was a great help in our situation that the way of salvation is described very clearly in this book, as well as the practical steps required for repentance and conversion. In our case, where conversion did not take place in the presence of an experienced Christian, the assistance provided by the book, even an already formulated prayer which we used as a guide, was very important. We also became aware of the importance of belonging to a Bible-based church. We have now joined a free evangelical congregation in Lemgo.

Carola and Lutz Meyer (Kalletal, Germany, aged 25 and 34 respectively)

Getting your name in the "Book of Life"

... how does this happen? Or: How do we board the lifeboat?

You will have noticed from the above personal testimonies that each of them was in a different situation before coming to saving faith. Every person's life is unique, just as all snowflakes are different. There can never be two life stories that are the same, we have one significant thing in common when we leave the ship of death and board the lifeboat, namely that we are now assured of salvation. The practical details of the transfer are now discussed.

When we wish to turn to Jesus Christ, we can know that He is already expecting us: "Here I am! I stand at the door and knock. If anyone hears my voice and opens the door, I will come in" (Rev 3:20). First of all we should pray to Jesus to forgive all our sins. Such a prayer[1] could for example go like this:

[1] **About prayer:** If we want to tell somebody something, then we do it in our own words and according to our own individual style of speech. When praying to Jesus for salvation, we do exactly the same. A personal conversation with God and Jesus Christ is known as prayer. We simply mention our request (desiring to be saved, or asking for forgiveness) and thank Him for the salvation promised in his Word. The prayers given here are definitely not fixed ritualistic formulas. Rather, they are possible examples. You, the reader, should pray in your own words, according to your own situation. If you are inexperienced and do not know how and what to pray, you may use the examples as your own prayer, after familiarising yourself with the contents.

"Lord Jesus, it has now become clear to me who You are. I know that God created this world and all life through You. You also made me – my body with all its many functions. You have given me my sense organs for observing the world, as well as my soul and spirit for knowing You. I believe that You are the Son of God and that You were nailed to the cross on Calvary, where You died on account of my sins – all my actions and thoughts which are sinful in your eyes, and make me guilty before You. Because You were completely sinless, death could not hold You. You arose from the grave and live now. You are the great Lord over all things! I pray now for You to also be my personal Lord and Master.

I know that with the guilt of my life's sin, I cannot for one moment stand before You and the living God in the place of judgement. But You came into this world to save lost sinners. Your death on the cross was the price paid for me so that I might go free and not be punished. In that fact I trust. My entire life is an open book before You. You know all the errors of my ways, every false inclination of my heart, and my previous indifference towards You. So now I ask You – please, take away all my guilt before You and forgive all my sins; everything that I can think of, as well as everything that doesn't come to mind right now. Take all those things away from me. I thank You that You are doing that right now. You are the Truth, therefore I trust the promises in Your Word. Amen."

Now you have done what we read in 1 John 1:9: "If we confess our sins, He is faithful and just and will forgive us our sins and purify us from all unrighteousness." There are two very important matters from this fundamental verse which we need to take to heart and emphasise:

135

1 Certainty: Jesus is faithful, meaning that He always keeps his promise to forgive the sins of anybody who prays for remission. We do not always do what we say, but anything Jesus has promised is forever certain. All your transgressions have now been pardoned. If you were to doubt this, something evil would have transpired: you would be calling Jesus a liar. But if you believe that you have now received forgiveness, then you honour the Lord Jesus Christ (possibly for the very first time). Through this, you acknowledge what He said about Himself: "I am the truth" (John 14:6). The certainty of pardon is so exceptionally important for a true conversion, that Peter emphasises: "For you *know* that it was not with perishable things such as silver or gold that you were redeemed,... but with the precious blood of Christ" (1 Peter 1:18-19). The word *know* is crucial. God now commands us to go forth secure in the knowledge of forgiveness.

2 All sin is removed: Note the very important last two words of 1 John 1:9: He will "purify us from all unrighteousness". Imagine for a moment that this sentence included a statement that He would purify us from 99.999 % of our sins. Let us follow this through logically. If I were to die tonight, would I go to heaven? Of course not, because 0.001 % of our sins would be enough to be barred from heaven. God does not allow the faintest taint of sin in His heaven. That is why we have to be cleansed 100 %, as this passage asserts. He takes all our sins away – everything from childhood to the present day, including sins which are still hidden.

But what about tomorrow and the day after? Will we then be totally free from sin? Or can sin again enter our life so that evil starts all over? Does this mean that the present thoroughgoing pardon is worthless? These questions deserve answers.

Eternal life becomes ours at conversion. At the same time our earthly life is changed; it is now characterised by a radical break with sin. This can be illustrated as follows in railway terminology: "Before our conversion, when we sin, we are completely 'on track', but afterwards, every sinful act or thought is like a railway accident, a derail-ment from our new path." A saved person is set "free from the law of sin and death" (Rom 8:2). He no longer needs to sin. Even a converted person will not live a totally sin-free life, but the status of sin has changed completely. Accidents are not included in a railway timetable, but they do happen. In such a case the authorities investigate the rails, the signalling system, the technical equipment of the train, and the conduct of the engine-driver. Everything possible is done to prevent a repetition. It is the same in the case of sin. War has now been declared on sin (read for example 1 John 3:7-10 and Hebr 12:4).

This new life also finds expression in a changed way of life. Those who have found peace with God will reflect this in their present life. Not only do we ourselves benefit from this change, but also those around us. The epistle to the Colossians strikingly compares this change to the taking off of an old garment and putting on a new one.

"But now you must rid yourselves of all such things as these: anger, rage, malice, slander and filthy language from your lips. Do not lie to each other, since you have taken off your old self with its practices and have put on the new self, which is being renewed in knowledge in the image of its Creator... Therefore, as God's chosen people, holy and dearly loved, clothe yourselves with compassion, kindness, humility, gentleness and patience. Bear with each other and forgive whatever grievances you may have against one another. Forgive as the Lord forgave you. And over all these virtues put on love, which binds them all together in perfect unity. Let the peace of Christ rule in your hearts, ... Let the word of Christ dwell in you richly" (Col 3:8-16).

After you have been released from all your sins at the foot of the cross, you can then ask Jesus to come into your life. Do not fear that He will somehow exploit you. There are many historical examples of people being enslaved, deceived, exploited and abused by their kings, emperors and political leaders. Not so in the case of Jesus. He is the good Shepherd who loves us more than anybody else could love us. Of Himself He said: "The good shepherd lays down his life for the sheep... I am the good shepherd; I know my sheep and my sheep know me... My sheep listen to my voice; I know them, and they follow me. I give them eternal life" (John 10:11, 14, 27, 28). He wants to guide our life in the best way; He brings us to the Father and gives us heaven as a gift. So you should hand your entire life completely over to Him. Give Him more space than just a fifty-fifty share; all aspects of your life must belong to Him, and you will be richly blessed. This is the one and only way to become a child of God. One does not qualify through membership of a church in which one was born and raised, neither will any good deed, or being baptised as a baby, ensure that you become a child of God. The only way is by making a deliberate decision to come to Jesus, beginning with a prayer. This second prayer can be formulated along the following lines, modified according to your thoughts and preferences:

"Now, dear Lord Jesus, I pray that You will enter my life. Lead me along the way which You will show me through my reading of the Bible and by means of your guidance in my life. I know that You are the Good Shepherd and that You always intend the best for me. I therefore entrust You with all areas of my life. I don't want you to be a mere sailor on the ship of my life, I want you to be the Captain. You know all the rocks and currents which might wreck my life. Please steer my ship throughout my life. I entrust everything to you: My thoughts and acts, my career, my leisure time, my plans, my finances, my health, my illnesses, my joys, my worries ... Grant me the power to make a clean break with my previous sinful life. And if I stumble now and then, let me recognise these immediately as mishaps and confess them immediately to You. Please order my life and give me new habits involving You, under your blessing. Change my disposition towards You and the people I come across. Make my heart obedient to You and please open the Bible for me so that I may correctly understand your Word. I want to acknowledge You as Lord of my life and to follow You from now on. I wish to stay close to You. Amen."

What has now happened? If this prayer, or a similar one freely composed by you, has been sincere and really came out of your heart, then you have just become a child of God. This is not human wisdom, but God Himself confirms it: "to all who received him (Jesus), to those who believed in his name, he gave the right to become children of God" (John 1:12). Something great has now happened, and this is a very important day in your life, even if you perhaps cannot realise it at the moment. The step you took today, is compared in the Bible to being born (a rebirth, since you have already been born physically). This day of your decision has eternal significance. You have received the whole of heaven as a gift.

Eternal life is now yours. Nobody can take away from you what Jesus earned for you and has just now given you as a gift. God is not your Judge anymore, but has become your Father, and He now sees you as being free from sin, as if you have never sinned in your life. The whole of heaven took part in this momentous event of your conversion. One person has left the ship of death and has boarded the lifeboat. Jesus says of this in Luke 15:10: "I tell you, there is rejoicing in the presence of the angels of God over one sinner who repents." In heaven it is not important which team wins the world series, who steps onto the winner's podium at the Olympic Games, or when the President of the USA holds a meeting with another world leader. But the fact that you have found the way to your eternal home resounds throughout heaven with great joy. Recently, when I asked somebody after his conversion what was happening in heaven right now, he replied spontaneously: Joy, a thousand times over!

The Holy Spirit has now also entered into you. He plays an important role in your life. It is He Who testifies in your heart that you are a child of God (Rom 8:16). He assures you that God's Word is true and He guides you deeper into Scripture. Jesus calls the Holy Spirit "the Spirit of truth" (John 14:17).

Now you can be quite certain that you have been accepted by the living God as His child – you have been adopted into the family of God. Did you give or pay anything for this privilege? No, you have received everything as a gift; the Bible calls this grace. What does a child say when receiving a piece of chocolate? Thank you! You should do this, too, because God has given you the whole of heaven as a gift. Here, too, a short example of a prayer of gratitude may be helpful:

"Dear Father in heaven, You have now become my Father, and I can now be your child. You have freed me from all sin and guilt through your Son, the Lord Jesus Christ. Lord Jesus, I thank You that You have saved me also. Amen."

Now the fulfilled life, which God promises, begins. In the Bible your present state is regarded as being like that of a newborn baby. Just as a newborn already belongs to a family, you now belong to the family of God. Newborn babies are in a critical stage of life – think of sudden infant death syndrome, for instance. This is also possible in the realm of faith. The birth (conversion) has been successful, resulting in real new life. At this stage nourishment (milk) and good care are essential. Naturally, here too, God has provided. He has done everything necessary for you to be able to develop properly. "Infant death" is avoidable by following God's directions. Your spiritual development will be healthy and sound if you take the following five points to heart:

1 Reading the Bible: Your decision was based on the words of the Bible, which is the only book authorised by God. No other book can compare in regard to authority, truth, wealth of information, and source. Reading this Word is essential nourishment for your new life. This aspect is expressed clearly in 1 Peter 2:2: "Like newborn babies, crave pure spiritual milk, so that by it you may grow up in your salvation." The words of the Bible are this milk. To be informed of the will of God, you should cultivate the habit of reading the Bible daily. The best place to start is with one of the gospels; John is especially suitable. Do not begin with the books of Deuteronomy or with Ezra. When learning mathematics, one does not start with integral calculus. This is something for

later, after mastering the essentials. You should make it a beloved daily habit to read something in the Bible. We don't forget breakfast or brushing our teeth, because these activities have a fixed place in our daily rhythm; we should be just as consistent about the Bible.

2 Prayer: Just as we speak to people whom we encounter in our daily familiar surroundings, like our marriage partner, our business colleagues, neighbours and friends, so we should also speak to God, as we are reminded in Colossians 4:2: "Devote yourselves to prayer." According to the Bible prayers can only be addressed in one of two ways: To God (Col 4:3) Who is now your Father, and to the Lord Jesus (Col 2:6-7) Who is your Saviour, your Good Shepherd, and your Friend – yes, your everything. Prayers to any other person (or thing) people might suggest are unbiblical. Being merely human inventions, they do not arise from the will of God. If you have previously been accustomed to directing your prayers elsewhere, discard such practices immediately, so that you might not act contrary to God's declared will.

Prayer will change you, and you will find abundant power through prayer. All everyday matters can be prayed for; all your joys and worries, plans and intentions. Thank the Lord for everything that concerns you, and pray for the needs of others around you, especially that they would also come to a living faith. Bible reading and prayer comprise a "spiritual circulation" which is essential for a healthy life of faith.

3 Communion: We have been created to have fellowship with others. Seek out and cultivate contact with other true Christians. Note that many people call themselves Christians, but you are required to have fellowship with born-again believers. You will find that you can only really pray and converse with true believers. When a glowing coal is removed from the fire, it dies quickly. Our love for Christ will also cool off if it is not kept burning through fellowship with other born-again Christians.

Check out the church into which you were perhaps born, or which you are thinking of now attending, to make sure that the entire Word of God is believed. This cannot be taken for granted, especially these days. If they teach that one must be converted in order to be saved, then that is a good sign. But if these sorts of words never feature, and they concentrate only or mainly on political, ecological and social matters, then stay away – there is "death in the pot" (see 2 Kings 4:40). Leave such a place; traditions cannot save us, no matter how venerable. Rather, join a fellowship which is faithful to the Bible, and become active there. A good, lively congregation, where the entire Bible is believed, is an essential prerequisite for our faith and for a healthy spiritual growth. Take very careful note of this point number three, because many have withered here, although they once made a genuine profession of faith.

4 Obedience: When reading the Bible, you will find many helpful instructions for all realms of life and also for communion with God. If you practise what you have learned, you will find great blessings. The best way to express our love for God, is to obey Him: "This is love for God: to obey his commands" (1 John 5:3).

5 Witnessing: You are now safe and secure in the lifeboat. The ship of death cannot pull you down into the abyss any more, but many people are still travelling on the doomed ship. You should now help many of them to board the lifeboat. Tell others what Jesus Christ means for you. People who have not yet accepted the saving truth of the gospel, require our example and testimony. You are now a fellow-worker of God (1 Cor 3:9). Jesus emphasises the meaning of personal witnessing in Matthew 10:32-33: "Whoever acknowledges me before men, I will also acknowledge him before my Father in heaven. But whoever disowns me before men, I will disown him before my Father in heaven." The Thessalonian believers set the correct example in this respect: "The Lord's message rang out from you not only in Macedonia and Achaia – your faith in God has become known everywhere" (1 Thess 1:8).

You should rejoice that you have deliberately turned to Jesus Christ and have been accepted by God. The priorities in your life have now been rearranged, with the interests of God's kingdom playing the central role. The believer hungers after the words of God and he seeks fellowship with other Christians. He is led by the Holy Spirit (Rom 8:14), and the fruits of the new life will become obvious to everybody: "But the fruit of the Spirit is love, joy, peace, patience, kindness, goodness, faithfulness" (Gal 5:22).

At conversion, the old life immediately ends and the new one begins. The New Testament expresses it this way: "If anyone is in Christ, he is a new creation" (2 Cor 5:17). Through conversion two things are achieved: our present earthly life acquires a new, central meaning and purpose, and at the same time, we receive the gift of being a child of God, entitling us to be His heirs, to inherit eternal life.

Every believer.

The well-known verse John 3:16, was once called the pole star of the Bible by the evangelist C. H. Spurgeon. It affirms the love of God for all people: "For God so loved the world that he gave his one and only Son, that whoever believes in Him, shall not perish but have eternal life." We could also put it like this: Nobody lives his life on this earth without being loved by God. God is kind towards us, because He loves us. Through this goodness He calls us to believe: "do you show contempt for the riches of his kindness, tolerance and patience, not realising that God's kindness leads you towards repentance?" (Rom 2:4; Greek: *metanoia* = conversion, about-face, changing one's mind).

In his famous home-coming drama *Draußen vor der Tür* ("Outside the door") the German poet, Wolfgang Borchert, (1921 – 1947) described the neediness and loneliness of the survivors of the Second World War. One notable scene involves a dialogue between God and Beckmann, a soldier returning home from Russia, wearing gas mask goggles.

God: People call me the loving God.

Beckmann: Funny, that. They must be very strange people to call you that. They must be the contented, the satisfied, the happy ones, and those who are afraid of You. Those who walk in sunlight, are in love, are sated or content ...

God: My child, my poor –

Beckmann: ... Where were You actually, dear loving God, when the bombs roared? Or were you loving when eleven of my reconnaissance patrol went missing? Eleven men too few, dear God, and You weren't even there, dear God. These eleven men must have cried aloud in the lonely forest, but You were simply not there, dear and loving God. Were You loving in Stalingrad, dear God, were You loving there? How were you loving there? Yes, how? When did You ever really love, God, when? When did You ever care about us, God?

God: Nobody believes in me any more. Not you, not anybody. I am the God in whom nobody believes any more. And nobody is concerned with me anymore. You don't care about me, either.

Beckmann: ... Oh, but You're old, God, You're not modern, not with it, You can't really cope any more with our fears or our long lists of casualties. We don't really know You any more, You are a fairy-tale God of love – today we need a new one. You know, one for our fears and needs. A completely new one. Yes, we have sought You all right, God, looked for You in every ruin, in every shell-crater, in every night of darkness. We have called You. God!!! We have screamed out for You, wept, cursed! Where were You then, dear and loving God?

God: My children have turned away from me; I did not turn from them. You turned away from me; you, from me. I am the God in whom nobody believes any more. All of you have turned away.

Man in heaven: sharing the glory of Jesus

A student approached me after a presentation in the city of Mainz, Germany. I noticed her determination to get an answer as she said, *"You've just been talking about time and life after death. But what is eternity exactly?"* I was surprised to be asked this question by such an attractive young woman. She was so full of life, why didn't she just postpone the question as many other people do? I said to her, *"I'm interested to know why this question is so important to you."* She replied, *"I was recently diagnosed as having a hereditary heart condition. As it stands, the doctors have given me just a few more years to live. So you see, I have to know what eternity is."*

I immediately realized that this was neither a theoretical, nor a quibbling theological question, but a very existential one. I was moved by the clarity and decisiveness with which this young woman was looking for an answer to this fundamental question. Before I could answer her she made it clear what she didn't want to hear.

She said, *"I can imagine what hell is like. I have read Sartre, and he described it in one piece quite evocatively: people are locked in a room and cannot understand each other. They can never leave the room. Never. That is hell. I can imagine that. But what is heaven like? That is what I would like to know."* She continued, *"And please don't tell me it 'll be singing Hallelujah or praising God unendingly. I can't imagine having to sing forever. Nor do I desire to praise God continually for the rest of eternity. But I know eternity is our goal in life. It has to be something I can look forward to."*

I tried, in my answer, to describe heaven as a place full of joy and love. She interrupted me right away, *"That is not precise enough for me. How could I rejoice in a place where there is nothing but joy? One can only feel joy as such when one has experienced its opposite, sadness or anger."*

The young woman challenged me to examine the question more intensively and to answer exactly, according to the Bible. I will never forget that conversation, as it led me to shift the focus of my presentations to the theme of heaven. What a blessing it would be if more people asked such specific questions about life after death!

At the end of our conversation, she said, *"Why is so little preached or written about eternity? Why do most sermons only deal with this life? People are being denied something crucial."* She was right, and because of that encounter in Mainz, I have included a chapter in this book which deals with the question of life after death in detail.

The young woman spoke of both heaven and hell. We, too, will deal with both places, as Jesus preached vigorously and repeatedly on both subjects.

What about hell?

During the Vietnam war, a minister went to comfort a dying soldier. The soldier knew he had only minutes left to live, only minutes before he would be faced with eternity. There was only one question burning in his soul: "Minister, is there a hell?" The minister's answer was a clear, "No." The soldier's reply was equally clear: "If there is no hell, then we don't need you here at all. You should just go home! But, if there really **is** a hell, then you've misled everyone you have spoken to. You're just lying to us here."

Jesus clearly speaks of hell as a place that exists. His intention is never to scare us, but to warn us and to invite us into the other, equally real place - heaven.

In the Sermon on the Mount, Jesus warns us: "If your right eye causes you to sin, gouge it out and throw it away. It is better for you to lose one part of your body than for your whole body to be thrown into hell. And if your right hand causes you to sin, cut it off and throw it away. It is better for you to lose one part of your body than for your whole body to go into hell" (Matt 5,29-30).

Let us take yet another passage from the Gospel of Matthew: "Do not be afraid of those who kill the body but cannot kill the soul. Rather, be afraid of the one who can destroy both soul and body in hell" (Matt 10:28). Who sends people to hell? It is certainly not the devil, although that might seem likely at first. The devil himself is condemned and will be judged (Rev 12:10; Rev 20:10). The Judge will make the Last Judgment, and God has set the Lord Jesus to be that Judge. As we read in Matthew 25:41: "Then he [= Jesus] will say to those on his left, 'Depart from me, you who are cursed, into the eternal fire prepared for the devil and his angels.'"

Towards whom are the warnings about hell directed? Who is being addressed? I always thought that they were directed at the faithless, the outsiders, the thieves and criminals. However, in almost all cases Jesus directs his warnings about hell towards the faithful. He only addresses the Pharisees on occasion, but when he does, Jesus is especially strict with them because of their self-righteousness. They do not receive a *warning*, because hell is a *certain* end for them: "Woe to you, teachers of the law and Pharisees, you hypocrites! You shut the kingdom of heaven in men's faces. You yourselves do not enter, nor will you let those enter who are trying to (Matt 23:13)."

The British author David Pawson once compiled a list of those deeds which, according to the Bible, lead to hell. This list contains 120 points and names, among others, the following groups of people:

- the adulterers
- the homosexuals
- the debauched
- the liars
- the miserly
- the proud
- those who follow astrology
- the cowardly
- the slothful
- ...

In the Parable of the Talents, the man who receives one talent says: "Master, ... I knew that you are a hard man, harvesting where you have not sown and gathering where you have not scattered seed. So I was afraid and went out and hid your talent in the ground. See, here is what belongs to you" (Matt 25:24-25). His Lord answers him, "You wicked, lazy servant! So you knew that I harvest where I have not sown and gather where I have not scattered seed?" (Matt 25:26). The text ends with the punishment of rejection: "And throw that worthless servant outside, into the darkness, where there will be weeping and gnashing of teeth" (Matt 25:30). The Bible defines this place of darkness as hell. This servant is neither an atheist, nor a bad person in the usual sense. He is one who knows Jesus. That is why he addresses Jesus as "Master." Despite this, he is lost. And why? Because he is lazy!

In the Sermon on the Mount, Jesus gives a serious warning to those who habitually have his name on their lips, but will never see the glory of God: "Not everyone who says to me 'Lord, Lord' will enter the kingdom of heaven, but only he who does the will of my Father who is in heaven" (Matt 7:21). The Parable of the Ten Virgins is also about the faithful. But five of them were to find that "the door was shut" (Matt 25:10). Why? Their way of life reflected more the customs of the time than the Commandments of God, and Jesus Christ was no longer the centre of their lives. That is why they hear the unexpected words of Jesus: "I tell you the truth, I don't know you" (Matt 25:12).

144

On the third of June 1998, possibly the most tragic railway accident in the history of Germany occurred when a broken wheel caused a high-speed train ICE to derail and slam into a concrete bridge in the small town of Eschede near Hannover. One hundred people died in that accident. On the twenty-first of June, a funeral service for the victims was held in Celle, with the President and the Chancellor of Germany both in attendance, as well as the friends and families of the victims. Of course, in a situation like this, a sermon should offer comfort and support to the relatives. However, the sermon should still be truthful. Both Catholic and Protestant clergy preached that the victims of the accident would all go to heaven. That is not right. We do not know how many of the deceased really knew the Lord Jesus. It would surely be a percentage similar to that among people in our neighbourhood and at our place of work. Unfortunately, there are only few who have truly taken the Lord Jesus into their lives. According to the Bible, only they will be received into heaven (John 3:3).

In a similar situation involving an accident at the time of Jesus, he comments on those on whom the tower of Siloam fell (Luke 13:4). Jesus' answer is worth noting: "But unless you repent, you too will all perish" (Luke 13:5). He uses the event not to bless the dead, but to preach to the living.

One preacher writes: "People used to be afraid of hell. Today, they are afraid of talking about it." One can only speak of being saved where there is danger to be saved from. Because there is a hell, we need a saviour. This saviour is the Lord Jesus: "For God did not send his son into the world to condemn the world, **but to save the world through him** [= Jesus]" (John 3:17). Jesus Himself is the gate to heaven: "I am the gate; whoever enters through me will be saved" (John 10:9).

What do we know about heaven?

The following quip about heaven is from the German poet Heinrich Heine (1797 – 1856): "We shall let the angels and sparrows have heaven" (from *Wintermärchen*). Hopefully, he changed his mind after he had written that line, or he is regretting his eternal isolation in the place of darkness.

Heaven as a concept is used in many sayings and forms of speech to describe various aspects of life. When one is happy, one is "in seventh heaven." Something that is very good is "heavenly." There is even a delicious flavour of ice cream called "Heavenly Hash." For most people the only knowledge they have about heaven is what they hear in everyday expressions like that. Is that all that there is to say about heaven?

So what do we know about heaven?

On closer examination it becomes clear that the idioms fall far short of a satisfactory description of heaven. God has revealed a number of specific details about heaven to us. The Bible is the only authoritative source of information – anything else is pure speculation and the product of human imagination. The Bible often addresses this topic which is the greatest goal given to mankind. Numerous aspects of heaven become clear when we read the Word of God and apply reason to the understanding of it. In our study we will occasionally refer to relevant aspects of our life here on earth for comparison.

While we can test whether the Bible is right about earthly things, we have to accept what it says about heaven in faith. That is why Jesus said, "I have spoken to you of earthly things and you do not believe; how then will you believe if I speak of heavenly things?" (John 3:12).

It is impossible to grasp that this eternal and almighty God would like to share our company in heaven. He sends His servants to invite all peoples and nations until all are in attendance: "Then the master told his servant, 'Go out to the roads and country lanes and make them come in, so that my house will be full' " (Luke 14:23).

We have been given an unmistakable description of the way to heaven so that we don't miss this greatest of opportunities. Jesus states in John 14:6: "No one comes to the Father except through me". This word is fulfilled in heaven. Only those people who have been saved by the Lord Jesus will reach heaven (John 3:36; 1 John 5:13).

In the ten points which follow we will look at the nature of heaven in more detail.

1 Heaven is the place where we will be perfectly happy

The French philosopher Jean Jacques Rousseau (1712 – 1778) does not get at the heart of the meaning of happiness when he remarks that "happiness is having a healthy bank account, a good cook and excellent digestion." Voltaire (1694 – 1778) states that "total happiness cannot be known, it is not created for man." This philosopher is also wrong. Jesus can make us really happy. When Jesus talks about being happy, or blessed, it means much more than what we understand by the word 'happy' today. The eternal component is important. Jesus saw his main task as saving humans (Matt 18:11). Those who are saved are happy because they are given the glory of heaven. This supreme happiness begins here on earth and will be perfected in heaven: "Therefore he is able to save completely those who come to God through him" (Hebr 7:25). Only those who are saved know real joy and happiness.

In heaven, the place without sin, happiness will be perfect and everlasting, for none of the negative aspects of this world will tarnish life there.

Many people must bear unspeakable suffering on this earth. The bookshelves of the world are full of accounts of suffering and innumerable questions as to why an almighty and loving God can allow them to happen.

Ever since the Flood, humanity has not remained immune to catastrophes, large and small. On the first of November 1755, an earthquake in Portugal turned Lisbon into a pile of rubble. Sixty thousand people died. This event did not fit into the view of the world held by most people at the time. Greatly moved and critical, the German author Goethe wrote, "God the Creator and

Keeper of Heaven and Earth did not show himself to be fatherly in his punishment of both the righteous and unrighteous."

There is no shortage of accounts of terrible suffering. The high number of victims does not matter, whether six million or sixty thousand. The death of even one person is enough for us to ask: "How could God allow this to happen?" In the life after death, all traces of suffering will be erased. There, nothing will remind us of pain, war, hate or death. "He will wipe every tear from their eyes. There will be no more death or mourning or crying or pain, for the old order of things has passed away" (Rev 21:4).

Our body will then be freed from all disease and frailty. It will never have to fight with germs, viruses, infections, diseases of the heart or lungs. There will be no such things as hospitals or prisons. There will be no more need for doctors, nurses, police officers, prison wardens or gravediggers.

Once we are in heaven, nobody will want to return to earth. The time of burdens and worries will be over forever.

The Prussian king Frederick the Great (1712 – 1786) named his castle in the city of Potsdam near Berlin *Sanssoussi* (without worries) but led a life full of worries. *Sanssoussi* would only be a correct description of heaven. Heaven is the only place where there is no fighting, no war, no hate, no unfaithfulness, no worries and no broken hearts.

2 Heaven is a place of pleasure for the senses

We humans pay a lot of money just to be able to see or hear something special.

– Outrageous prices are paid to be at the opening ceremonies of the Olympics, for example. At the 1996 Summer Games in Atlanta, tickets cost over one thousand dollars each, not to mention the even more inflated prices of the ticket scalpers.
– The concerts of famous conductors are popular among those who wish to treat their ears to

146

something special. The first night performances of plays are just as sought-after.
- For tennis or football fans, the finals in Wimbledon or the Superbowl game are a special treat.

All that we now consider attractive, beautiful to look at or a pleasure to hear pales in comparison to heaven. The Bible describes both the wisdom of God as well as heaven fittingly when it says: "No eye has seen, no ear has heard, no mind has conceived what God has prepared for those who love him" (1 Cor 2:9).

Not just our eyes and ears but all our senses will be satisfied in heaven. That includes for example, our tastebuds but also much, much more – everything that makes us feel good will be available in heaven: love, peace, joy, friendliness, goodness.

3 Heaven is the place of everlasting celebration

How do we prepare for a celebration? The yearly presentation of Oscars took place in Los Angeles on March 23 1998. It was a gala party of film, to which previous Oscar-winners, sponsors and many actors were invited. One magazine described the Oscar time-stress as follows:

"Pre-Oscar:
three months to go: book appointment with hairdresser
one month to go: visit spa
10 days to go: get hair cut
3 days to go: visit tanning salon

On Oscar Day:
morning: work out, shower, wash hair, eat light meal
lunch: wait for hair stylist
afternoon: wait for make-up artist
4pm exactly: guests must be in auditorium

Then the doors close. The dice have been cast. 'And the Oscar goes to...' "

As this example shows, the preparation for a celebration which only lasts a few hours can take

tremendous effort. Most of the effort is spent on beauty. In this world, everything deteriorates, and beauty fades. The effort to compensate with artificial means increases with age. None of this will be necessary in heaven. There we will all be beautiful. More precisely: we will all be *glorious*, and glorious is the superlative of beautiful.

Jesus is described even in the Old Testament when we read, "The Lord reigns, he is robed in majesty" (Ps 93:1). He is the "glorious Lord Jesus" (James 2:1). On his return, He will come in all His power and glory (Matt 24:30). In John 17:22, He prays to His Father: "I have given them the glory that you gave me."

God has a problem: How can He make us humans understand the glory and festivity of heaven? Jesus explains in a parable: "The kingdom of heaven is like a king who prepared a wedding banquet for his son" (Matt 22:2). A wedding is the most beautiful celebration on earth. Everything is prepared, down to the last detail:

- beloved guests are invited
- the best food and finest drink will be served
- no problems will be discussed on the special day
- the bride will look more beautiful than ever before, and will wear the most beautiful and most precious dress of her life
- everyone will have a good time

In using this well-known picture, Jesus tries to describe heaven to us as an unusually beautiful celebration. At the Last Supper, He says to His disciples: "I tell you, I will not drink of this fruit of the vine from now on until that day when I drink it anew with you in my Father's kingdom" (Matt 26:29). That wine will be like nothing we have ever tasted here on earth. I also believe we will eat in heaven. How else are we to interpret Luke 12:37: "He [= Jesus] will dress himself to serve, will have them recline at the table and will come and wait on them."

We can safely assume that it will be a richly set table. The earthly concepts of "costly" and "pre-

147

cious" are too weak to describe what we will find in heaven. But it is clear that heaven is festive.

Now comes the surprise: Heaven is not just comparable to a wedding, but is the place where a real wedding occurs. In Revelation 19:7 we read, "Let us rejoice and be glad and give him glory! For the wedding of the Lamb has come, and his bride has made herself ready." Jesus Himself is the groom, and all who have been saved through Him are the bride.

Those who are invited can consider themselves happy. In the Parable of the Lost Son, we read that "they began to celebrate" (Luke 15:24). Joy is everlasting in heaven; we cannot estimate the degree of this happiness.

4 Heaven is a beautiful place

Jesus said in the Sermon on the Mount, concerning this Creation, "See how the lilies of the field grow. They do not labor or spin. Yet I tell you that not even Solomon in all his splendor was dressed like one of these" (Matt 6:28-29). The creation displays the Creator's love of beauty which mankind cannot imitate. God is the originator of all that is beautiful.

After much suffering, God blessed Job: "And he also had seven sons and three daughters. The first daughter he named Jemimah [= little dove], the second Keziah [= cinnamon blossom] and the third Keren-Happuch [= precious vessel]" (Job 42:13-15). The beauty of Job's daughters is especially emphasized. They would have won any Miss World Competition.

Of Jesus Himself, the Creator in person, it is said in Psalm 45:2: "You are the most excellent of men and your lips have been anointed with grace, since God has blessed you for ever." When He is sacrificed on the cross for the sin of humanity, however, He gives up His beauty, as we can read in Isaiah 53:2, "He had no beauty or majesty to attract us to him, nothing in his appearance that we should desire him".

Jesus has always been described as beautiful and perfect. In Isaiah 33:17 it is written: "Your eyes will see the king in his beauty." The well-known German song *Fairest Lord Jesus* expresses this aspect especially well:

Fairest Lord Jesus, Ruler of all nature
O Thou of God and man the Son
Thee will I cherish
Thee will I honour
Thou my soul's glory, joy and crown.

Fair are the meadows, fairer still the woodlands
Robed in the blooming garb of spring
Jesus is fairer
Jesus is purer
Who makes the troubled heart to sing.

Fair is the sunshine, fairer still the moonlight
And fair the twinkling, starry host
Jesus shines brighter
Jesus shines purer
Than all the angels Heav'n can boast.

...

Beautiful Saviour! Lord of the nations!
Son of God and son of man!
Glory and honour,
Praise, adoration
Now and forevermore be thine.

(From the German "Schönster Herr Jesus", 1677)

If God's love for beauty is evident even in this Creation, in the form of every snowflake, each lily, orchid and the countless blooms of other flowers or the luxurious plumage of some birds, how much more fitting it is to have beauty as one of the most important attributes of heaven!

Many people seek beauty on this earth. Surgeons who perform facelifts are in great demand. An entire industry specializing in the making and selling of beauty-enhancing or beauty-preserving products is assured of thriving business. Yet, even the most renowned of this world's Beauty Queens will see their beauty fade. Everything on earth is perishable (Rom 8:20).

The Empress Elisabeth of Austria, better known by her nickname Sissi (1837 – 1898) was known in the 19th century as the most beautiful woman in Europe. She was so vain that she would not have her portrait painted after her thirtieth birthday, let alone have photographs taken of her. The German author Annelie Fried writes, "Female television hosts reach their date of expiry at the age of forty. After that, the nation watching from their living rooms counts the wrinkles."

Heaven, in contrast, is a place of everlasting beauty. All who have gone there will stay beautiful forever. When we become like Jesus (1 John 3:2), we will also receive His beauty. The earthly value of looking "forever young" is not nearly adequate to describe the heavenly ideal.

5 Heaven is where our lives will be fulfilled

Most of mankind live below the poverty line. Forty thousand children die daily because they do not have enough to eat. Others are rich; they can afford whatever worldly goods their heart desires and yet are unhappy. Many suffer from depression and worries, or are simply bored.

Jesus is aware of both emotional and physical human needs. "When he saw the crowds, he had compassion on them, because they were harassed and helpless, like sheep without a shepherd" (Matt 9:36). He wants to help especially here; that is why in John 10:10 He gives as the main reason of His Coming: "I have come that they may have life, and have it to the full."

Converting to Jesus changes our lives so fundamentally here on earth that we can clearly see the difference between the old and the new life (Rom 6:4; Col 2:6; 1 Pet 4:3). However, it is once we are in heaven, that our lives become completely fulfilled. There, we will know for the first time, what true quality of life means.

A critic once said that he would never feel like sitting on a cloud and playing a harp for ten thousand years. That is a fabricated picture of life after death, one which we do not find in the Bible.

Heaven is life in abundance. The concept of scarcity is not known in heaven. There is nothing there in need of improvement. Boredom is also unknown, for heaven is complete and offers a life of fulfillment.

While hell can be described as a place of lasting unfulfilled desires, there will be no more yearning in heaven. This does not necessarily mean that all our earthly desires will find their fulfillment in heaven, but that the richness of heaven will be shared with us – a richness which we cannot even imagine – a richness which will make earthly desires superfluous.

When we experience beautiful moments here on earth, we want to hold on to them. That is what Goethe describes when he writes, *"Stay but, thou art so fair!"* Cameras and videos capture the past; they do not represent life. Heaven, on the other hand, could be described as *everlasting simultaneousness*. Nothing is constrained by mortality. Everything is permanent.

Here on earth, we can only be in one place at one time. Each move brings separation from people we love. Saying "good-bye" is often painful. In heaven, we will never have to say "good-bye."

6 Heaven is a home for us

The architects of this world continually invent new types of buildings. Jörn Utzon, the architect of the Opera House in Sydney, Australia, used a peeled orange as his inspiration. We admire powerful palaces of glass and high-reaching towers of concrete. An architect once wrote that "architecture unites the demands of art with technical perfection. Architecture has been the expression of humanity's yearning for the eternal. Besides architectural works of genius, monuments such as the Great Wall of China and the Pyramids of Gizeh count as some of the longest-lasting works of human hands."

In a nineteenth-century spa resort on the North Sea island of Juist, a special building was reopened in 1998 after massive reconstruction. The *White Castle by the Sea*, as it is called, located

149

on a high dune, is the first sight on approaching the island by water. Besides the five-star hotel complete with ballroom, restaurant, children's play area and exclusive bar, private apartments are also available in the hotel at the astronomical price of approximately $US 850,000 for 80 m² (= 264 square feet). However, even the most luxurious apartments cannot offer both a sea view and bright sunlight. The apartments facing north have the sea view, but have no direct sunlight. If you want a sunny apartment you have to do without the sea view. Even in this amazingly beautiful, and expensive place you can't have everything.

After we die we will live in a home that was designed by Jesus. What the Creator of the world can build is something that no earthly architect could even dream of. Jesus says, in John 14:2-3, "In my Father's house are many rooms; if it were not so, I would have told you. And if I go and prepare a place for you, I will come back and take you to be with me that you also may be where I am."

Jesus has been building our home for over two thousand years. How beautiful it must be! Any earthly comforts provided in the spa resort of Juist will be superseded by our home in heaven. If, in this Creation, even every snowflake and each acorn leaf is unique, then how much more will this be true of homes built by Jesus! There is no repetition; everything is especially tailored for the person who will reside there. We have a place in heaven for ever, under a sun that never sets.

7 Heaven is a place where we shall reign

Heaven will be a place of singing and rejoicing for us, but we will also have duties: "And they will reign for ever and ever" (Rev 22:5).

In the Parable of the Ten Minas, described in Luke 19:11-27, each servant receives ten minas and is told to put this money to work. One servant increases the amount by ten, another by five. When Jesus judges, the first servant is told, "Well done, my good servant! ... Because you have been trustworthy in a very small matter, take charge of ten cities" (Luke 19:17). The second servant

receives, in turn, what he deserves, "You take charge of five cities" (Luke 19:19).

We may conclude that, after we die, the responsibility of reigning will be handed over to us. The assigned areas will not be equal in size, but will depend on how hard we have worked for God's Kingdom here on earth. In heaven, we will reign together with Jesus. We have a part in the ruling in eternity.

Here, politicians do everything and anything to get elected. The position of governing will be handed to us in heaven. This task will involve many creative and changing duties. Completing our duties will be easy, for there will be no job stress, no ladder to climb, and no politics in heaven.

8 Heaven is the place where Jesus is

Sometimes, historical meetings have wide-reaching consequences. For example, we owe the knowledge of how to make porcelain to the meeting of the physicist Tschirnhaus and the alchemist Johann Friedrich Böttger. Even today, something special can grow out of a surprise meeting, especially if God's hand is behind it. Two people who have never before met are brought together. They develop a common understanding about something and act accordingly, with significant consequences.

The one single meeting that has the most significant and wide-reaching consequences is when a person meets with God. That person then finds everlasting life in Jesus. The Bible mentions many such meetings. Zacchaeus, the corrupt chief tax collector of Jericho, changed his way of life and became a believer (Luke 19:1-10). The finance officer of Ethiopia was looking for God in Jerusalem and found Him in the desert. Only after becoming secure in the knowledge of his salvation, does he go on his way, rejoicing (Acts 8:26-39). Saul became Paul through Jesus. Once a persecutor of Christians, Paul became the most important missionary of all time (Acts 26:12-18). In the same way, everyone can meet Jesus uniquely, if we approach Him with openness. Those who dare to meet Him are rewarded with entry into heaven.

Jesus prays to His Father in John 17:24, "Father, I want those you have given me to be with me where I am." This prayer is fulfilled in heaven. We will be with Him for all eternity. When faith is fully revealed it will be replaced by wonder. When the queen of Sheba arrived at the court of Solomon she cried in surprise, "Indeed, not even half... was told me" (2 Chron 9:6). This expression of surprise will be even more fitting when we arrive in God's kingdom. Here, on earth, there are still many pressing questions, to which we seek answers. There, with Jesus, everything will be explained: "In that day you will no longer ask me anything" (John 16:23).

"There will be no more night" in the presence of God and Jesus (Rev 22:5). We will no longer need sleep, therefore we will not need beds in heaven. The sun will shine forever. Yet it is not a celestial body which will provide the light. No created sun will shine for eternity, but "the glory of God gives it light, and the Lamb is its lamp [= Jesus]" (Rev 21:23). Isaiah saw the everlasting sun prophetically in God's kingdom: "The sun will no more be your light by day, nor will the brightness of the moon shine on you, for the LORD will be your everlasting light, and your God will be your glory. Your sun will never set again" (Is 60:19-20).

Thousands of people flock to overflowing beaches in their holidays to soak in the glowing sun most of them get nothing more than sunburn and have to live with the danger of skin cancer, worrying whether or not the SPF of their sunblock lotions is high enough to screen out harmful rays. However the everlasting sun of heaven will be good for us and will never burn. It will not be the scorching sun we know in the deserts of this earth (Rev 7:16).

9 Heaven is where we become like Jesus

I hardly dare to say it, but it is written in 1 John 3:2: "Dear friends, now we are children of God, and what we will be has not yet been made known. But we know that when he appears, **we shall be like him.**"

What does that mean? Man was created in the image of God, but this identity was lost in the Fall. The Bible is referring to Jesus when it says that, "the Son is the radiance of God's glory and the exact representation of his being" (Hebr 1:3). If in heaven we become like Jesus, then we too will be the radiance of God's glory and the exact representation of His being.

Individually, we will have our unique personalities, but our qualitative physical traits (beauty, glory, figure, physical perfection) will be that of Jesus (Phil 3:21). That body will not be restricted by time or space (John 20:19).

Here on earth, it is very rare that we meet someone who shares our thoughts and beliefs. But when this does happen, we cherish these conversations and time seems to fly. That which is said is stimulating and enriching, usually leading us to new discoveries which we would not have made but for the other person's input.

In heaven, we will become one in thought with Jesus. Communication with Him will be an integral creative element. Even after all of our earthly questions have been answered, there will still be new and boundless things to contemplate. Just like the way that those dear to us want to get to know us as well as possible, we will want to get to know the inexhaustible kingdom of God (Is 40:28) and Jesus (Col 2:3). Right after the creation of man, God gave him the creative task of naming the animals (Gen 2:19-20). Does it not follow that the Lord in heaven will continue this creative conversation? Communication in heaven is not an exchange of knowledge with which we could fill an encyclopedia, but a continually enriching dialogue.

10 Heaven is something special to look forward to

In looking at the content of Jesus' words, one aspect is impossible to ignore. He continually invited us to heaven. He began his preaching with the words, "the time has come. The kingdom of God is near. Repent and believe the good news" (Mark 1:15). Jesus tried to describe heaven to us in many parables. "The kingdom of heaven is like

- a man who sowed good seed in his field" (Matt 13:24).
- a mustard seed" (Matt 13:31).
- yeast" (Matt 13:33).
- treasure hidden in a field" (Matt 13:44).
- a merchant looking for fine pearls" (Matt 13:45).
- a net" (Matt 13:47).
- a king who prepared a wedding banquet for his son" (Matt 22:2).

The soul-searching conversation with Zacchaeus ends with a reference to eternal salvation: "Today salvation has come to this house. ... For the Son of Man came to seek and to save what is lost" (Luke 19:9-10).

Jesus does not promise children an easy life on this earth, but he promises them heaven: "Let the little children come to me, and do not hinder them, for the kingdom of God belongs to such as these" (Luke 18:16).

When Jesus sees the paralytic he does not tell him first "Get up and walk!", but "Your sins are forgiven" (Matt 9:2). It is once again clear that a decisive freedom from sin is a prerequisite for heaven and is of the utmost importance to Jesus.

The Sermon on the Mount is so often misquoted today, but heaven is its main subject:

- "Blessed are those who are persecuted because of righteousness, for theirs is the kingdom of heaven" (Matt 5:10).
- "But seek first his kingdom and his righteousness and all these things will be given to you as well" (Matt 6:33).
- "Enter through the narrow gate. For wide is the gate and broad is the road that leads to destruction, and many enter through it. But small is the gate and narrow the road that leads to life, and only a few find it" (Matt 7:13-14).

As the disciples returned from a missionary journey, they rejoiced to know that even the demons submitted to them. Jesus reminded them that they had a much greater reason to rejoice, "Do not rejoice that the spirits submit to you, but rejoice that your names are written in heaven" (Luke 10:20). Jesus gives absolute priority to this particular reason for joy. 1 Peter 1:8 refers to this, saying: Rejoice "with an inexpressible and glorious joy."

If we show the way to glory to just one other person, it will result in insurmountable joy in heaven: "In the same way, I tell you, there is rejoicing in the presence of the angels of God over one sinner who repents" (Luke 15:10).

This means:

- The most important task God's children have is to spread the word that will lead people to heaven. This heavenly assignment still has utmost priority.

- Until the return of Jesus, the eternal goal must remain the main topic of biblical preaching and pastoral care.

- Knowing that we have a home in heaven (Phil 3:20) should form the substance of our lives and infect others with our joy.

Abbreviations used for the books of the Bible

Books of the Old Testament (OT)

Gen	Genesis	Eccl	Ecclesiastes
Ex	Exodus	Song	Song of Solomon
Lev	Leviticus	Is	Isaiah
Num	Numbers	Jer	Jeremiah
Deut	Deuteronomy	Lam	Lamentations
Jos	Joshua	Ez	Ezekiel
Judg	Judges	Dan	Daniel
Ruth	Ruth	Hos	Hosea
1 Sam	1 Samuel	Joel	Joel
2 Sam	2 Samuel	Amos	Amos
1 Kings	1 Kings	Ob	Obadiah
2 Kings	2 Kings	Jonah	Jonah
1 Chr	1 Chronicles	Mic	Micah
2 Chr	2 Chronicles	Nah	Nahum
Ezra	Ezra	Hab	Habakkuk
Neh	Nehemiah	Zeph	Zephaniah
Esth	Esther	Hag	Haggai
Job	Job	Zech	Zechariah
Ps	Psalms	Mal	Malachi
Prov	Proverbs		

Books of the New Testament (NT)

Matt	Matthew	1 Tim	1 Timothy
Mark	Mark	2 Tim	2 Timothy
Luke	Luke	Tit	Titus
John	John	Phlm	Philemon
Acts	Acts	Hebr	Hebrews
Rom	Romans	Jam	James
1 Cor	1 Corinthians	1 Peter	1 Peter
2 Cor	2 Corinthians	2 Peter	2 Peter
Gal	Galatians	1 John	1 John
Eph	Ephesians	2 John	2 John
Phil	Philippians	3 John	3 John
Col	Colossians	Jude	Jude
1 Thes	1 Thessalonians	Rev	Revelation
2 Thes	2 Thessalonians		

Technical bibliography

Ulrich Drews:
Taschenatlas der Embryologie
Georg Thieme Verlag Stuttgart, New York
1st Edition 1993, 386 p.

Adolf Faller, Michael Schünke:
Der Körper des Menschen
Georg Thieme Verlag Stuttgart
8th Auflage 1978, 452 p.

Heinz Feneis:
Anatomisches Bildwörterbuch
Georg Thieme Verlag Stuttgart, New York
5th Edition 1982, 451 p.

Rainer Flindt:
Biologie in Zahlen
Gustav Fischer Verlag, Stuttgart, New York
2nd Edition 1986, 280 p.

Rainer Klinke, Stefan Silbernagel:
Lehrbuch der Physiologie
Georg Thieme Verlag Stuttgart, New York
1st Edition 1994, 808 p.

Alfred Moelicke (Ed.):
Vom Reiz der Sinne
VCH Verlagsges. mbH, Weinheim
1st Edition 1990, 217 p.

Mörike, Betz, Mergenthaler:
Biologie des Menschen
Quelle & Meyer Verlag, Heidelberg, Wiesbaden
13th Edition, 817 p.

Robert F. Schmidt (Ed.):
Grundriß der Sinnesphysiologie
Springer Verlag, Berlin, Heidelberg, New York
4th Edition 1980, 336 p.

Stefan Silbernagl, Agamemnon Despopoulos:
Taschenatlas der Physiologie
Georg Thieme Verlag Stuttgart, New York
4th Edition 1991, 371 p.

Also various journal articles.

© Copyrights and acknowledgements:

Medical illustrations:
Raimar Glatz, Bergneustadt

Cartoon illustrations:
Carsten Gitt, Braunschweig

Microphotograph (page 56):
Manfred P Kage / Bildagentur Okapia, Frankfurt

Photographs and compositions:
Dieter Otten, Gummersbach

About the author:

Prof Dr Werner Gitt was born in Raineck, East Prussia (Germany), on the 22nd of February 1937. He studied at the Technical University in Hannover from 1963 to 1968 and obtained a degree in engineering. From 1968 to 1971 he was an assistant at the Institute for Control Technology of the Technical University, Aachen. He obtained his doctorate after two years' research. In 1971 he was appointed head of the Data Processing Division (now: Information Technology) of the Federal Institute for Physics and Technology (Physikalisch-Technische Bundesanstalt, PTB) in Braunschweig (Brunswick). In 1978 he was promoted to Director and Professor at the PTB. His research concerns have involved information science, mathematics, and systems control technology. His many original research findings have been published in scientific journals or have been the subject of papers presented at scientific conferences and at universities at home and abroad. In addition to his professional activities, he is much engaged with the Bible and related topics. He has written numerous publications on Bible-and-science matters, on which he has also given many lectures, both in Germany and abroad (e. g. Australia, Austria, Belgium, France, Hungary, Kazakhstan, Kirgizskaya, Lithuania, Namibia, Norway, Poland, Portugal, Roumania, Russia, South Africa, Sweden, Switzerland, and the USA). Most of these talks were strongly evangelistic. He married his wife Marion in 1966; Carsten was born in September 1967, and Rona in April 1969.

155

Other books by the author (and available in English):

In the Beginning was Information
CLV Bielefeld, 1st English edition 1997, 256 p.
(2nd German edition 1994, 288 p.)

Did God Use Evolution?
CLV Bielefeld, 1st English edition 1993, 152 p.
(4th German edition 1994, 159 p.)

Stars and their Purpose: Signposts in Space
CLV Bielefeld, 1st English edition 1996, 217 p.
(2nd German edition 1995, 222 p.)

If Animals Could Talk
CLV Bielefeld, 1st English edition 1994, 127 p.
(11th German edition 1999, 122 p.)

What About the Other Religions?
CLV Bielefeld, 1st English edition 1995, 159 p.
(6th German edition 1997, 160 p.)

Questions I Have Always Wanted to Ask
CLV Bielefeld, 2nd English edition 1998, 192 p.
(15th German edition 1998, 192 p.)

Addresses for ordering these books:

Worldwide: CLV Bielefeld,
PO Box 110135,
D-33661 Bielefeld, Germany

Australia: *Answers in Genesis*,
PO Box 6302, Acacia Ridge DC, Qld 4110

USA: *Answers in Genesis*, PO Box 6330, Florence,
Kentucky 41022